Once-a-Month Cooking

Revised Edition

❏

Once-a-Month Cooking

REVISED EDITION

Mimi Wilson and
Mary Beth Lagerborg

St. Martin's Griffin ✖ New York

ONCE-A-MONTH COOKING, REVISED EDITION. Copyright © 1999 by Mimi Wilson and Mary Beth Lagerborg. All rights resrved. Printed in the United States of America. No part of this book may be used or reproduced in any manner whatsoever without written permission except in the case of brief quotations embodied in critical articles or reviews. For information address St. Martin's Press, 175 Fifth Avenue, New York, N.Y. 10010.

Library of Congress Cataloging-in-Publication Data

Wilson, Marilyn S.
    Once-a-month cooking / Mimi Wilson and Mary Beth Lager-borg.—Rev. ed.
      p. cm.
    ISBN 0-312-24318-9
    1. Make-ahead cookery.   2. Low-fat diet—Recipes.   I. Lager-borg, Mary Beth.   II. Title
TX652.W5647   1999
641.5'55—dc21   99-30057
                                       CIP

Design by Songhee Kim

10 9 8 7 6 5 4 3

❏

To our most expert—and honest—recipe testers: Calvin Wilson; Kurt and Lori Wilson; Tom and Kyndra Trinidad; Kevin Wilson; and to Alex Lagerborg; Tim Lagerborg; Dan Lagerborg; and Andrew Lagerborg.

❏

ACKNOWLEDGMENTS

❑

Our warmest thanks to family and friends who have contributed recipes, table-talk questions, and their perspective to this edition of *Once-a-Month Cooking:* Anne Gates; Kurt Wilson; Lori Wilson; Renee Loring; Sue Herd; Cynthia Bahlman; Capt. Lois True; Ginger Brown; Linnea Rein; Sandi Hanson; Cala Doolittle; Marge Rodemer; and Alice Tate.

CONTENTS

❑

Introduction

❏

"What's for dinner?" is the perennial, pesky question that compels you to examine this book. You might have tonight covered, but your family's need to eat—best yet, to eat together—comes in relentless waves.

And you have things to do besides cook! *Once-a-Month Cooking* is a method for people who don't always want to cook, but want to have cooked. You are smart and you understand that nothing unravels the seams of quality family time faster than having nothing on hand for dinner. Not having clean laundry runs a distant second.

Once-a-Month Cooking is a method of cooking a month's (or two weeks') dinner entrées at a time and freezing them. Yes, of course it works! (That's the question we're asked most often. Although a couple who cook this way were featured in the *National Enquirer*, it is seriously not outrageous.)

You don't have to be particularly organized nor a good cook to do this. You don't need a separate freezer. You don't need a Tupperware distributorship, although a drawerful of Tupperware will help.

We will take you by the hand and give you a shopping list and lots of direction. We'll tell you what size containers to freeze the food in and suggest what to serve with your entrées. When you're finished, gazing into your well-stocked freezer will be a near-spiritual experience. Afterward, on any given day you can cook from scratch if you want to, but if you don't have time—no problem. This is a great way to simplify your life, relieving it of the daily stress of what to fix for dinner.

The beauty of *Once-a-Month Cooking* is that it provides the convenience of a home-meal replacement with the aroma, appeal, taste, nutrition, and cost savings of home cooking. For the investment of one large grocery haul and a day of megacooking, you have a month's (or two weeks') entrées available on time each day with little effort on your part beyond reheating a meal in the oven and steaming vegetables or tossing a salad. And you don't need to dash out for fast food, Chinese takeout or go to the neighborhood deli.

This system will save you money. Convenience foods are costly. So are forays into the supermarket at 5:00 P.M. with two preschoolers. A list that began with four items yields a cart holding twenty-two, including Fruit Loops and Big Chew gum. With *Once-a-Month Cooking* you will have one large shopping trip a month (or every two weeks); then you'll only have to shop perhaps once a week for fresh produce, breakfasts, and lunches.

A bonus from your day's cooking investment is your flexibility. Having guests is more fun when the main dish is ready in advance. Your family can still have a home-cooked meal even if you are busy, have a new baby at home, when the holidays approach, or if you are traveling. What a joy it is to be able to respond to the special needs of your family and others!

We all know that nutrition fares better when we aren't eating catch-as-catch-can. And if you or another family member is on a special diet, *Once-a-Month Cooking* is an excellent way to feed the rest of the tribe.

You may want to try the two-week plan rather than the one-month plan if you are cooking in bulk for the first time, or if your family is small (fewer than four people). In that case, two week's worth will last you three weeks since you'll package it in smaller containers.

But the greatest benefit of *Once-a-Month Cooking* is that it gives you a better shot at pulling the family together—at least a few evenings a week—to disengage from the concerns of the world and engage with one another. A warm meal on a set table wafts the aroma of care and value to a family. As one mom said, "When the food is ready, and we're gathered at the table, the rest of the craziness doesn't seem to matter."

Home-meal replacements make it too easy for a family to separate, grab the meal when each family member wants, and see to his or her own needs. *Once-a-Month Cooking* will help you have a meal to gather round. Share the kitchen chores as well as your mealtimes together.

Once we're at the table it's discouraging to fall into the same conversation ruts about work or teachers, or how a child has misbehaved today. With our own families and friends we've found it's helpful and fun to sometimes "put a question on the table." We ask a question that each person at the table must address, but for which there is no right or wrong answer, such as "What is the funniest thing you saw today?"; "What is your favorite room of our home and why?"; "If you were an animal rather than a person, what animal would you like to be?" We've included table-talk questions to prime the pump for you. Turn off the television, ignore the telephone, and enjoy what you will learn about one another.

Mimi Wilson devised this cooking system to meet the daily needs of a busy family who entertained often. In the years since then, we have been encouraged and sometimes amused by the many uses people have found for, as we call it, "the method." Here are some that stretch beyond the obvious feeding of a busy family. Perhaps they will expand your vision for how you can use the wealth of food you will soon have on hand.

- Freeze individual portions to stock the freezer of an elderly parent or friend.
- Develop this as an at-home business to serve busy, two-income families. A day-care provider uses *Once-a-Month Cooking* so that for a fee, parents can pick up a dinner entrée with their child!

- Cook the method with friends in a church or community kitchen and use the entrées to take to families in crisis.
- Give entrées as a gift for a new mother or for a woman experiencing a difficult pregnancy.

We can't resist sharing our two personal favorite applications. On a visit to Peru, Mimi's husband Calvin, a family physician, was part of a medical team that trekked into the jungle to treat a group of people suffering from pneumonia. When the team needed additional food, Mimi took frozen entrées, packaged in Tupperware and wrapped in newspapers, to a nearby airstrip. The pilot flew over the team's campsite in the jungle and dropped the entrées to them. We call this one "Bombs Away."

The second application involves a letter we received. We receive many letters (and phone calls on cooking day). Some users actually say the results have saved their marriages. One user said she accomplished cooking this way although her past cooking catastrophes had put a person in the hospital and included things like frying a chicken in Tide. This one is a favorite:

> *Dear Madam,*
> *I ordered the book* Once-a-Month Cooking . . .
> *As a bachelor, I have cooked in bulk for years, though my menu consists of only one or two items.*
> *I am interested in mail-order bulk-food distributors. Do you have some addresses I could try?*
> *Thanks for your time,*
> *Dave Listoe*
> *North Pole, Alaska*

Whatever your impulse for trying *Once-a-Month Cooking,* we trust you'll find generous rewards for your day's cooking.

If you have used the previous edition of *Once-a-Month Cooking,* you will find in this edition a new two-week cycle of recipes, a few recipe substitutions in the other menu cycles, and general fine-tuning.

Are you ready to win the contest to have meals on hand? On your mark. Get set. Let the adventure begin!

❑

A Few Words from the Coaches: Cooking the Once-a-Month Way

❑

WARMING UP: AN OVERVIEW OF THE ONCE-A-MONTH PLAN

This cooking method enables you to prepare either a month or two weeks' main dishes at once and freeze them. It includes two choices of one-month cycles and three choices of two-week cycles. If you rotate among these, you can easily provide great mealtime variety. We suggest that you start with a cycle from the book to get used to the method. Then you can experiment with adding family-favorite recipes. Turn to Chapter 9 for help in adapting the method to your own recipes.

Each of the menu cycles gives you a menu calendar that shows the month's entrées at a glance, a grocery shopping list, a list of staples you should have on hand (so you can buy any you don't have), a list of the containers you will need for freezing the entrées, step-by-step instructions for preparing the recipes in sequence on your cooking day, and finally the recipes themselves in the order you will prepare them.

To serve an entrée, you will need to thaw the dish and heat it. While it is being heated, you can prepare a vegetable, salad, or perhaps a dessert to serve with it. The time-consuming preparation and cleanup is done all at once on your megacooking day!

Since many of the entrées can be frozen in freezer bags instead of bulkier hard-sided containers, even a month's cycle can be stored in the freezer section of your refrigerator. Just make sure you make room in it by cleaning it out before your cooking day. Sooner or later we need to deal with those hard knots of leftovers anyway! Right after cooking day you will probably not have room in the refrigerator's freezer for things like ice cream and loaves of bread, but as you use entrées from the freezer you can add these to it.

The recipes in *Once-a-Month Cooking* come not from stainless-steel test kitchens, but have been tested numerous times in homes by cooks of varying skills. We have selected recipes we think your family will eat and enjoy. They were chosen for taste, variety, nutritional value, easily available ingredients, and how well they lend themselves to freezing.

One of the two-week cycles consists entirely of low-fat entrées, selected in consultation with a dietitian. You may adjust the other menu cycles for low fat, for example by using soups and dairy products with reduced-fat content.

You will find that the recipes vary in serving size. The average is 5 or 6 servings. Some serve 4; a few serve 12. Depending on the ages (and eating habits) of your children, if you have four or fewer family members, you may want to divide and freeze each larger-serving entrée in two or more meal-size portions. The largest recipes are great for serving to company or ensuring leftovers the following day.

You may find that the one-month menu cycle actually feeds your family for five weeks or six or more—particularly if you occasionally eat out or supplement your menu with dinner salads or easy meals like grilled meats and vegetables.

Chapter 8 gives some of our favorite bread, breakfast, dessert, salad, and vegetable recipes to serve with your entrées.

Consult Chapter 10 for helpful information on such things as freezing tips and food-measurement equivalents.

AT THE STARTING LINE

Are you ready to cook? Or at least ready to THINK about getting ready to cook? Let us provide some tips to streamline the process.

First, read this introductory material. Then choose which menu cycle you would like to try this month and read through that chapter so you'll know what's ahead.

Next comes the hardest part: marking off the time on your calendar to grocery shop and cook. But if you don't do this, you won't accomplish *Once-a-Month Cooking.* These should be on adjacent days. Don't try to shop and cook on the same day, especially if you have young children, or you won't like us very much! You simply won't have the time or energy to do both. You might also not like us about four hours into your cooking day, when your feet are complaining and every pot and pan you own is dirty. But we are consoled by the thought that you will like us VERY MUCH when you peek at your larder, carefully labeled and layered in your freezer, as well as each day thereafter at about 5:00 P.M. The one-month cycles require about (of course this varies with the cook) a nine-hour day. The two-week cycles take about four to five hours.

Cook with a friend or your spouse or an older child. The day goes so much more quickly when you divide the work and add conversation. If you have young children, a cooking companion can help tend the kids, answer the phone, and wipe the counters. You can either divide the food between your two families or cook one day a month at your friend's home and one day a month at your own.

Trust us that you will want to go out to dinner on cooking day. Yes, we know you will have plenty on hand for dinner. But you won't want to face any of it on your plate. This will pass. Go out, then have your spouse and kids wash the pots and pans.

Err to the side of buying a little more produce, chicken, and ground beef than is called for on your shopping lists. You can always use these for salads, soups, and sandwiches. If you have chicken broth left over, freeze it in an ice-cube tray. When the cubes are frozen, pop them in a freezer bag. You can pull out a cube when a recipe calls for chicken broth, or make spur-of-the-moment chicken soup with leftovers.

You may want to photocopy the recipes and attach them to large index cards. In many cases you will be working on more than one recipe at a time. You can lay out your recipe cards in sequence to save you from having to keep turning the pages.

Don't even think about trying to do extra baking on your cooking day. If you enjoy making pie crust and want to use your own rather than a store-bought one, prepare the pie crust a couple of days ahead.

Finally, although you need to free yourself of commitments on your cooking day, the day will go much more easily if you feel free to take a break to tend to the children's needs, make a phone call, or just sit down to rest! Wear supportive shoes. Listen to your favorite music. Crack open a kitchen window for ventilation and to let the good smells pour out.

The secret of the method involves *doing all similar processes at once*: browning ground beef and chopping onions and cooking chicken only once rather than several times a month. Imagine the hours this saves!

GROCERY SHOPPING HINTS

Before you go to the supermarket, read the grocery and staples lists for the menu cycle you plan to use. The staples list contains items you need but probably have on hand. Look through your cupboards and add any missing staple items to the grocery shopping list. Also check the list of suggested freezer containers to see if you need to buy any of them.

For added convenience, photocopy the grocery list that we provide; then write in the other staple items or containers you'll need to buy. The grocery lists have been categorized by sections of food to help speed you through the store.

If you shop for the one-month menu cycle, you will have to push one cart and pull another. You may need to budget more carefully in order to set aside the funds needed to purchase food for all your dinner entrées at once. But keep in mind that over the course of the month you will save money on your food bill by cooking this way, since you'll be buying in bulk, eating out less often, and eliminating unplanned trips to the supermarket.

Your shopping trip will take you a couple of hours, so don't try to wedge it between two appointments. If you take young children, be sure to go when everyone is well fed and rested. It also helps to break up the trip. For example, go midmorning to a discount food store to buy in bulk, have lunch at a favorite spot, and then finish any leftover shopping at the supermarket. Since this will be a lengthy shopping trip, plan your route through the supermarket so you visit the meat and dairy aisles last. If a friend or relative can baby-sit for you on shopping day, you will accomplish more in less time.

When you get home from shopping, you don't have to put everything away. Stack the canned goods and dry ingredients on a table or counter because you'll be using them soon. Keeping them within sight can inspire you for the task ahead!

The grocery shopping lists include some items with asterisks (*). These can be stored because you will not need them until the day you serve the corresponding entrée. Mark the labels of these items to remind you not to use them by mistake. For example, mark an X across a soup label, package of rice or spaghetti, or on a plastic bag holding a fresh tomato.

THE DAY BEFORE COOKING DAY

After you've returned from the grocery store, clear off the kitchen counters, removing any appliances you won't be using. Create as much free countertop space as you can. Then, following the "Equipment Needed for Cooking Day" list, pull out your food processor, mixer, bowls—the tools you will need. If you have room, you may also want to get out the staple items.

Make sure you have all needed groceries on hand. Then perform the tasks that your chosen menu cycle outlines for "The Day Before Cooking Day."

If you don't have a food processor to chop and slice the vegetables, you may want to cut them up the day before cooking since this is one of the most time-consuming tasks. Then store these vegetables (except mushrooms) in the refrigerator in cold water inside tightly sealed plastic containers. Or omit the water and seal them in zip-closure bags.

Finally, check the list of freezer containers needed for the entrées in your menu cycle and get out the ones you'll need. You can usually store entrées in freezer bags unless they are layered (like lasagna) or contain a lot of liquid. Food stored in freezer bags can be thawed in the bag and then warmed in a suitable container.

COOKING DAY

The assembly order for each menu cycle is a step-by-step guide to preparing all your entrées. Read through the assembly order before you start to cook. Since you will usually be working on more than one recipe at a time, getting an overview will give you a sense of how the steps flow together.

The following suggestions will help make this method work best for you:

- Place an empty trash can in the center of the kitchen, and corral the pets where they won't be underfoot. You'll want to avoid wasted motion wherever possible on cooking day.
- Use a timer—or two timers—to remind you something is in the oven or boiling for a certain length of time.
- Pause to wash pots and pans as necessary. Washing dishes and wiping up periodically as you work will help you work more efficiently and make end-of-the-day cleanup easier.
- If you sauté several food items in succession, use the same skillet. Sometimes you'll only need to wipe it out and put in the next ingredients. Put a Crock-Pot to work by using it overnight for brisket, for example, and then for soup or stew on cooking day.
- Set frequently used spices along the back of the stove or on a nearby counter. Use one set of measuring cups and spoons for wet ingredients and another for dry. That way you'll need to wash them less often.
- You will *perform all similar tasks at once.* For example, do all the grating, chopping, and slicing of the carrots, celery, cheese, and onions. Set them aside in separate bowls or plastic bags. Cook all the chicken if you didn't do that the day before. Brown all the ground beef and sauté all the onions at one time. These tasks may seem tedious, but you will have accomplished a lot when you're finished, and assembling the dishes will go much faster.

At the close of your cooking day, save leftover sliced or diced vegetables and cooked meat for a soup, a salad, or for snacks.

FOOD STORAGE AND FREEZER TIPS

As you complete recipes, set them aside on a table to cool. When two or three have cooled, label each with the name of the entrée, the date you prepared it, and reheating instructions so you won't have to consult the recipe when you are preparing to serve it. For example:

> Aztec Quiche
> 10/8
> Bake uncov. 40–50 mins. at 325°

If a recipe calls for cheese to be sprinkled on top the last few minutes of baking, pour the grated cheese in a small freezer bag. Then tape the bag to the side or top of the corresponding entrée's container so that you are freezing the two together.

Make the best use of your 13x11x2-inch baking dishes. Spray a dish with nonstick spray, line the dish with heavy aluminum foil, seal the entrée, and freeze it. When the entrée has frozen completely, remove it in the foil and return it to the freezer.

When sealing food for freezing, remove as much air from the container as possible and seal it airtight. This will help guard against the cardboardlike taste called freezer burn. When using freezer bags, label the bag with an indelible marker before you insert the food.

Post the menu of foods you've prepared on your freezer or inside a cupboard door to help you choose each day's dinner and to keep an inventory of what entrées you've used. Check off the dishes as you serve them. For the freshest taste, seal containers airtight and use them within a month to six weeks. (For additional freezer storage tips, see Chapter 10.)

SERVING SUGGESTIONS

Remember each evening to pull the next night's entrée from the freezer and put it in the refrigerator to thaw. If the food is in a freezer bag, set the bag in a casserole dish to thaw, in case any liquid leaks out. You can also thaw the dish in the microwave the next day. Use the rule of thumb that by 9:00 A.M. you'll have decided what you'll serve for dinner that night.

Each recipe includes suggestions for salads or vegetables you might serve with the entrée. You'll find some of those recipes in Chapter 8. Now that you've saved time on your entrées, try some new salads, vegetables, or desserts, whether you have company or the same familiar faces around your table.

You'll spend less time in the kitchen during the coming weeks. You will save time, money, and energy you can invest in many other ways. Imagine how good it will feel to have entrées on hand, and to have an immediate answer to each day's nagging question "What's for dinner?"

Let's get cooking!

EQUIPMENT NEEDED FOR COOKING DAY

On cooking day, you'll want to reuse bowls and pans as much as possible to conserve counter and stove-top space. The following equipment will be needed:

Appliances
        Blender or hand mixer (for The Cross Country plan)
        Crock-Pot (for the first one-month and two-week plans)
        Food processor or grater

Pots, Pans, and Skillets

1 extra-large pot, canning kettle, or 2 large pots (to cook chickens)

2 large pots, one with lid

1 large saucepan with lid

1 medium saucepan with lid

1 small saucepan

1 large skillet

1 medium skillet

1 rimmed baking sheet (for The Long Jump plan); 2 rimmed baking sheets (low-fat plan)

Bowls and Containers

1 set of large, medium, and small mixing bowls

8 to 12 small-to-medium bowls or plastic bags (for grated, sliced, or chopped ingredients)

Miscellaneous Tools

Can opener

Colander

Cutting board

Hot pads

Kitchen scissors

Knives (cutting and paring)

Ladle

2 sets measuring cups (one for wet ingredients and one for dry)

2 sets measuring spoons

Metal or plastic serving spatula

Mixing spoons

Rolling pin

Rubber gloves (for deboning chicken and mixing food)

Rubber spatula

Tongs

Vegetable peeler

Wire whisk

❏

CHAPTER 2

The Dash: A Two-Week Entrée Plan

❏

GROCERY SHOPPING AND STAPLES LISTS

An asterisk (*) after an item indicates it can be stored until you cook the dish with which it will be served. For example, the spaghetti will not be cooked until the day you serve Spaghetti. Mark those items with an X as a reminder that you will need them for an entrée.

When entrées require perishable foods to be refrigerated until served, you may want to use those dishes right away or buy the food the week you plan to prepare the dish. For example, fresh mushrooms would spoil by the end of a month.

For the two-week entrée plan, you will need these food items as well as the ones in the staples list that follows:

Grocery Shopping List

Canned Goods
    1 4-ounce can chopped, green chilies
    2 10¾-ounce cans condensed cream of mushroom soup
    1 10¾-ounce can condensed cream of chicken soup
    1 12-ounce can evaporated skim milk
    1 8-ounce and 2 4-ounce cans mushroom stems and pieces

THE DASH:
A TWO-WEEK ENTRÉE PLAN

SUN.	MON.	TUES.	WED.	THURS.	FRI.	SAT.
		1 Eat Out Cooking Day!	2 Chicken Packets	3 Mexican Stroganoff	4 French Bread Pizza	5 Calzones
6 Chili Verde	7 Spaghetti	8 Wild Rice Chicken	9 Balkan Meatballs	10 Marinated Flank Steak	11 Chicken Broccoli	12 Linguine à la Anne
13 Chili Hamburgers	14 Baked Eggs	15 Poulet de France	16	17	18	19
20	21	22	23	24	25	26
27	28	29	30			

1 11½-ounce jar salsa*

3 28-ounce cans Italian-style or plain crushed tomatoes in puree

1 12-ounce can tomato paste

1 8-ounce can sliced water chestnuts

Grains, Noodles, and Rice

4 hamburger buns

6 bread slices

1 loaf unsliced French bread (not sourdough)*

2 cups (about) seasoned croutons (1 cup croutons, ½ cup and ⅓ cup crushed crouton crumbs)

1 12-ounce package linguine

1 dozen corn tortillas*

1 8-ounce and 1 12-ounce package wide egg noodles*

8 ounces (1¼ cups) dry pinto beans

1 16-ounce package spaghetti*

1 12-ounce package seasoned bread stuffing—7-pound bird size (6 cups)

1 6¼-ounce package long grain and wild rice (Uncle Ben's Fast Cooking Long Grain and Wild Rice, if available)

Frozen Foods

1 10-ounce package frozen, chopped broccoli

2 loaves frozen bread dough (Italian, French, or pizza if available, otherwise wheat)

Dairy Products

9 eggs

¾ cup margarine

10 ounces (2½ cups) grated, mild cheddar cheese

10 ounces (2½ cups; 1 cup will be saved) grated mozzarella cheese*

4 ounces (1 cup) grated, low-fat Monterey Jack cheese*

4 ounces (1 cup) grated Parmesan cheese

2 ounces (½ cup) Romano cheese

1 3-ounce package cream cheese

1 8-ounce carton sour cream or plain low-fat yogurt*

2 packages refrigerated crescent rolls*

7 cups milk (whole, 2%, or skim)

Note: See Chapter 10 for ounce/cup equivalent measures.

Meat and Poultry

10 pounds whole chickens or 8 pounds chicken breasts

1 pound boneless, skinless chicken breasts

1⅔ pounds cooked ham
2 pounds lean ground beef (or substitute ground turkey)
1 pound bulk Italian sausage
1⅓ pounds flank steak
½ of a 3-ounce package of sliced pepperoni*
2 pounds round steak
½ pound ground turkey

Produce

1 small bunch celery
8 cloves garlic
1½ pounds white or yellow onions
1 bunch fresh parsley
2 green bell peppers and 1 red bell pepper (or 3 green bell peppers)

Staples List

Make sure you have the following staples on hand; add those you don't have to your shopping list.

allspice, ground
basil leaves, dried
bay leaves (4)
black pepper
cayenne pepper
chili powder (2 tablespoons)
chili sauce (½ cup plus 1 tablespoon)
chopped chives (¼ cup plus 1 tablespoon)
cloves, ground
cumin, ground
curry powder
flour, all-purpose (¼ cup plus 1 tablespoon)
ginger, ground
light mayonnaise (2 cups)
minced onion
nonstick spray
nutmet, ground
oregano leaves, dried
paprika
red wine (1 cup)
salt
seasoned salt
sherry (¼ cup)

soy sauce (¼ cup plus 1 teaspoon)
sugar
vegetable oil (1 cup)
waxed paper
Worcestershire sauce (2 teaspoons)

FREEZER CONTAINERS

The following list of freezer containers or flat baking dishes will be needed for the entrées in the two-week cycle. They're not the only containers in which you could freeze these foods, but the list gives you an idea of the size and number of containers you'll need.

10 Sandwich Bags
Calzones

11 1-Quart Freezer Bags
Chicken Packets (2); French Bread Pizza (3); Poulet de France; Linguine à la Anne (2); Calzones (2); Chili Verde

6 1-Gallon Freezer Bags
Wild Rice Chicken; Calzones (2); Balkan Meatballs; Chili Hamburgers; Marinated Flank Steak

1 3-Cup Container
French Bread Pizza

1 4-Cup Container
Spaghetti Sauce

1 5-Cup Container
Chili Verde

1 6-Cup Container
Mexican Stroganoff

3 13x9x2-Inch Baking Dishes
Poulet de France; Baked Eggs; Linguine à la Anne

1 7x11x2-Inch Baking Dish
Chicken Broccoli

Heavy Aluminum Foil
French Bread Pizza

THE DAY BEFORE COOKING DAY

1. Freeze the 4 hamburger buns in a plastic bag and the French bread in heavy foil, with the package of pepperoni taped to the foil. Refrigerate crescent rolls.
2. Cut 1 pound boneless, skinless chicken breasts into 1-inch cubes with kitchen scissors for Chili Verdes; refrigerate until needed.
3. In a large pot (or two), place the 10 pounds of whole chickens (or 8 pounds of breasts) in about 3 quarts water, making sure they're completely covered. Heat to a boil; reduce heat. Cover and simmer until thickest pieces are done, about 45 minutes to 1 hour. Save and refrigerate 6⅓ cups chicken broth; discard remaining broth or use for soup.

   Cool chicken until ready to handle; remove skin and debone. Cut into bite-size pieces with kitchen scissors, which are easier to use than a knife. Refrigerate chicken pieces in two plastic bags.
4. Set out appliances, bowls, canned goods, dry ingredients, freezer containers, and recipes.
5. Thaw 2 loaves of frozen baking dough in the refrigerator overnight.
6. Rinse pinto beans; cover with water and soak overnight.

COOKING DAY ASSEMBLY ORDER

Make sure you've cleared the table and counters of unnecessary kitchenware to allow plenty of working room. It also helps to have fresh, damp washcloths and towels for wiping your hands and the cooking area. The day will go a lot more smoothly if you keep cleaning and organizing as you work.

Before you prepare a recipe, gather all the spices and ingredients in the assembly area to save time and steps. When you finish the recipe, remove unneeded items and wipe off the work space.

Slightly undercook regular rice and noodles (al dente) that will be frozen. When you reheat them, they'll have a better consistency and won't turn mushy.

BEFORE ASSEMBLING DISHES

1. Cook and stir the bulk Italian sausage until brown in a large pot to be used for Spaghetti Sauce. Take a minute after chopping the onions, garlic, and parsley to complete Spaghetti Sauce according to the recipe. Start sauce boiling on the front burner, reduce heat, and then move pan to a back burner for 2 hours of simmering.
2. Perform all the chopping, grating, and slicing tasks:
   Onions: Finely chop all (store in cold water in a container with a tight-fitting lid).
   Garlic: Mince 8 cloves.
   Parsley: Chop ½ cup.
   Celery: Finely chop 1½ cups.
   Green and red bell peppers: Chop ¼ cup plus 1 tablespoon green bell pepper; slice 1 green and 1 red pepper.
   Cheddar cheese: Grate all.
   Monterey Jack cheese: Grate all.
   Mozzarella cheese: Grate 4 ounces; slice 6 ounces.
   Croutons: Crush enough to make separate ½ cup and ⅓ cup crumbs.
3. Spray the pans or baking dishes that you will need with nonstick spray (check list of freezer containers on page 17).
4. As you assemble the chicken, ham, beef, and miscellaneous entrées, allow them to cool if necessary, put them in storage containers, and freeze them.

Assemble Chicken Dishes

1. Skim off and discard chicken fat from 6⅓ cups broth.
2. Start the Chili Verde.
3. Cook rice for Wild Rice Chicken according to package directions.
4. Make filling for Chicken Packets in a medium bowl (mixing with hands works best), put mixture in a bag, and freeze.
5. Assemble Wild Rice Chicken.
6. Start Poulet de France.
7. Start cooking 10-ounce package of frozen, chopped broccoli.
8. Finish assembling Poulet de France.
9. Assemble Chicken Broccoli.
10. Add chicken and spices to Chili Verde and simmer 10 more minutes.
11. Cool Spaghetti Sauce and freeze as directed in the recipe.
12. Freeze chicken dishes.

Assemble Ham Dishes

1. Dice 1⅔ pounds ham, placing 4 cups in one bowl and 1 cup in another.
2. Boil linguine according to package directions.

3. Assemble Baked Eggs.
4. Complete Linguine à la Anne.
5. Freeze ham dishes.

Assemble Beef Dishes

1. Prepare Calzones and freeze.
2. Cut round steak into bite-size pieces.
3. Combine ingredients for Mexican Stroganoff and start it simmering.
4. Assemble and broil Balkan Meatballs.
5. Prepare Marinated Flank Steak.
6. Prepare Chili Hamburger patties.
7. Freeze beef dishes.

RECIPES FOR THE TWO-WEEK ENTRÉE PLAN

Each recipe offers complete instructions on how to prepare the dish. Food items with an asterisk (*) won't be prepared until you serve the entrée. For recipes calling for oven baking, preheat oven for about 10 minutes.

"Summary of processes" gives a quick overview of foods that need to be chopped, diced, grated, or sliced. "Freeze in" tells what bags and containers will be needed to freeze each entrée. "Serve with" offers suggestions of foods to accompany the meal. Some of the recipes for those foods are included in Chapter 8; page numbers are indicated for easy reference. "Note" includes special instructions on how the entrée can be used in other ways.

Spaghetti Sauce

1 POUND BULK ITALIAN SAUSAGE

1½ CUPS FINELY CHOPPED ONION

1 12-OUNCE CAN TOMATO PASTE

3 28-OUNCE CANS ITALIAN-STYLE OR
PLAIN CRUSHED TOMATOES IN
PUREE

2 CUPS WATER

4 TEASPOONS MINCED GARLIC
(4 CLOVES)

4 BAY LEAVES

2 TABLESPOONS SUGAR

4 TEASPOONS DRIED BASIL LEAVES

2 TEASPOONS DRIED OREGANO LEAVES

4 TABLESPOONS CHOPPED FRESH
PARSLEY

2 TEASPOONS SALT

1 16-OUNCE PACKAGE SPAGHETTI*

In a large pot, cook and stir the bulk Italian sausage with the onion until the meat is brown, about 15 minutes. Drain the fat. Add remaining ingredients, except the spaghetti. Bring sauce to a boil; reduce heat. Partly cover and simmer for 2 hours, stirring occasionally. (If desired, simmer in a Crock-Pot instead of pot.) Makes 12 cups sauce.

After sauce has cooled, freeze 4 cups for Spaghetti and 3 cups for French Bread Pizza; divide remaining 5 cups sauce in half, and freeze in 2 1-quart bags for Calzones.

To prepare for serving Spaghetti, thaw sauce and heat in a medium saucepan. Cook noodles according to package directions, drain, and pour sauce over them.

Summary of processes: Chop: 1½ cups onion, 4 tablespoons parsley; mince 4 cloves garlic
Freeze in: 4-cup container, Spaghetti; 3-cup container, French Bread Pizza; 2 1-quart freezer bags, Calzones
Serve with: Fresh Baked Asparagus (page 151), Cheesy-Herb Bread (page 135)

Makes 6 servings

French Bread Pizza

1 LOAF UNSLICED FRENCH BREAD (NOT SOURDOUGH)*
3 CUPS SPAGHETTI SAUCE*
¼ CUP GRATED PARMESAN CHEESE*

1 CUP GRATED MOZZARELLA CHEESE*
3 OUNCES PEPPERONI SLICES (HALF A PACKAGE)*

This recipe is assembled on the day it's served. Put sauce in a 3-cup container, cheeses in 2 1-quart bags, pepperoni in 1-quart bag; wrap bread in heavy foil. Freeze them together.

To prepare for serving, thaw French bread, sauce, grated cheeses, and pepperoni. Set oven to broil and/or 550°F. Slice loaf of French bread in half lengthwise. Layer sauce, Parmesan cheese, pepperoni, and mozzarella cheese on each half. Place bread on baking sheet and put in oven. Broil until mozzarella is melted. Cut pizza into serving-size pieces.

Summary of processes: Grate 4 ounces mozzarella cheese
Freeze in: 3-cup container; 3 1-quart bags; foil for bread
Serve with: Waldorf salad

Makes 6 to 8 servings

Chili Verde

8 OUNCES DRY PINTO BEANS (1¼ CUPS)

1 POUND BONELESS, SKINLESS
   CHICKEN BREASTS

1 4-OUNCE CAN CHOPPED GREEN
   CHILIES

1 TEASPOON GROUND CUMIN

¾ TEASPOON DRIED OREGANO LEAVES

⅛ TEASPOON GROUND CLOVES

⅛ TEASPOON CAYENNE PEPPER

3 CUPS CHICKEN BROTH (HOMEMADE)

1 TEASPOON MINCED GARLIC (1 CLOVE)

1 TEASPOON SALT

⅔ CUP FINELY CHOPPED ONION

1 CUP GRATED LOW-FAT MONTEREY
   JACK CHEESE*

1 11½-OUNCE JAR SALSA*

1 DOZEN CORN TORTILLAS*

Rinse pinto beans, soak them in cold water overnight, then drain them. Cut chicken into 1-inch cubes; cook in a small amount of water until no longer pink, about 15 minutes. Combine chicken with chilies and seasonings; refrigerate until needed. At the same time, combine beans, chicken broth, garlic, salt, and onion in a large pot; bring to a boil. Reduce heat and simmer until beans are soft, about 1 hour. Add more water if necessary.

Combine chicken mixture with beans; simmer 10 more minutes. Cool and freeze. Grate cheese, put in a 1-quart bag, and attach it to the freezer container with the chili.

To serve, thaw chili and cheese. Simmer chili 30 minutes, stirring occasionally. Top chili with salsa and grated cheese; serve on warmed corn tortillas.

Summary of processes: Soak ½ pound pinto beans overnight; cut 1-pound boneless, skinless chicken into 1-inch cubes; chop ⅔ cup onion; grate 1 cup low-fat Monterey Jack cheese
Freeze in: 5-cup container; 1-quart bag
Serve with: Tossed green salad

Makes 5 servings

Wild Rice Chicken

1 6¼-OUNCE PACKAGE QUICK-COOKING,
   LONG GRAIN AND WILD RICE

1 CUP COOKED, CHOPPED CHICKEN

1 8-OUNCE CAN SLICED WATER
   CHESTNUTS, DRAINED

1 CUP FINELY CHOPPED CELERY

1¼ CUPS FINELY CHOPPED ONION

1 CUP LIGHT MAYONNAISE*

1 10¾-OUNCE CAN CONDENSED CREAM
   OF MUSHROOM SOUP*

Cook rice according to package directions. Combine rice with chopped chicken, water chestnuts, celery, and onion; put mixture in a 1-gallon freezer bag.

To prepare for serving, thaw rice and chicken mixture, remove from bag, and place in a 2½ quart baking dish. Preheat oven to 325°F. Stir mayonnaise and condensed cream of mushroom soup together, and spread over top of chicken. Bake covered for 1 hour.

Summary of processes: Chop 1 cup cooked chicken, 1 cup celery, and 1¼ cups onion
Freeze in: 1-gallon bag
Serve with: Cooked green beans, peach halves with cottage cheese topped with a maraschino cherry, and Blueberry Pie (page 144)

Makes 6 servings

Chicken Packets

2 CUPS COOKED, CHOPPED CHICKEN	SALT TO TASTE
1 3-OUNCE PACKAGE CREAM CHEESE, SOFTENED	½ CUP CRUSHED, SEASONED CROUTON CRUMBS*
1 TABLESPOON CHOPPED CHIVES	2 PACKAGES REFRIGERATED CRESCENT ROLLS*
2 TABLESPOONS MILK (WHOLE, 2%, OR SKIM)	¼ CUP MELTED MARGARINE*

Mix chicken, cream cheese, chives, milk, and salt in a medium bowl (mixing with hands works best) to make filling and store in a 1-quart freezer bag. Put crouton crumbs in another 1-quart bag, attach it to the bag of chicken filling, and freeze them. Refrigerate crescent rolls.

To prepare for serving, thaw chicken mixture. Preheat oven to 350°F. Unroll crescent rolls. Each tube will contain 4 rectangles of dough with diagonal perforations. Press dough along each perforation so the rectangle halves will not separate. Place about ¼ cup of chicken mixture into the center of each rectangle. Fold dough over the filling and pinch the edges to seal tightly. Dip each packet in melted margarine, and coat with crouton crumbs. Place packets on a baking sheet. Bake for 20 minutes or until golden brown. Packets are good either hot or cold. (Serve early in the month before date expires on crescent rolls.) Makes 8 packets.

Summary of processes: Chop 2 cups cooked chicken and 1 tablespoon chives
Freeze in: 2 1-quart bags
Serve with: Smoky Corn Chowder (page 149), baked apples stuffed with plump raisins
Note: These packets are a favorite with children.

Makes 4 to 6 servings

Poulet de France

1 12-OUNCE PACKAGE SEASONED BREAD STUFFING (6 CUPS)
2 TABLESPOONS MELTED MARGARINE
2 CUPS CHICKEN BROTH, DIVIDED
3 CUPS CHOPPED, COOKED CHICKEN
½ CUP FINELY CHOPPED ONION
¼ CUP MINCED CHIVES
½ CUP FINELY CHOPPED CELERY

½ CUP LIGHT MAYONNAISE
¾ TEASPOON SALT
2 EGGS
1½ CUPS MILK (WHOLE, 2%, OR SKIM)
1 10¾-OUNCE CAN CONDENSED CREAM OF MUSHROOM SOUP
½ CUP GRATED MILD CHEDDAR CHEESE

In a medium bowl, mix stuffing, melted margarine, and 1¼ cups chicken broth. Mix cooked chicken, the remaining ¾ cup broth, onion, chives, celery, mayonnaise, and salt in another bowl.

Spread half the stuffing in a 13x9x2-inch baking dish treated with nonstick spray. Spread chicken mixture over stuffing. Cover with remaining stuffing. Whisk eggs, milk, and soup in a large bowl. Pour sauce evenly over stuffing. Cover dish with foil and freeze. Put cheese in a small freezer bag, and attach it to dish.

To prepare for serving, thaw grated cheese and chicken dish. Bake covered in a preheated 325°F oven for 30 minutes. Remove foil, sprinkle with cheese, and continue to bake uncovered for 10 minutes more.

Summary of processes: Chop 3 cups cooked chicken, ½ cup onions, and ½ cup celery; mince ¼ cup chives; grate ½ cup mild cheddar cheese
Freeze in: 13x9x2-inch baking dish; 1-quart bag
Serve with: Cooked frozen peas, lemon gelatin with pears, Cranberry Tea (page 144)
Note: This is a super dish to take to a potluck dinner.

Makes 8 servings

Chicken Broccoli

1 10-OUNCE PACKAGE FROZEN, CHOPPED BROCCOLI
4 CUPS COOKED, CHOPPED CHICKEN
1 10¾-OUNCE CAN CONDENSED CREAM OF CHICKEN SOUP
½ CUP LOW-FAT MAYONNAISE

1 4-OUNCE CAN MUSHROOM STEMS AND PIECES, DRAINED
¼ TEASPOON CURRY POWDER
¾ CUP GRATED PARMESAN CHEESE, DIVIDED

Cook broccoli in boiling water according to package directions. Drain broccoli and spread it in a 7x11x2-inch baking dish. Mix chicken, soup, mayonnaise, mushrooms, curry powder, and ½ cup of the Parmesan cheese in a medium bowl. Spread chicken mixture over broccoli. Sprinkle the remaining ¼ cup Parmesan cheese over top. Cover dish with foil and freeze.

To prepare for serving, thaw dish, and bake covered in a preheated 350°F oven for 40 minutes. Remove foil, stir to bring colder food in center to the outside; bake 20 minutes more.

Summary of processes: Chop 4 cups cooked chicken
Freeze in: 7x11x2-inch baking dish
Serve with: Croissants, Cranberry Cream Salad (page 147)

Makes 6 servings

Baked Eggs

6 BREAD SLICES, WITH CRUSTS REMOVED AND CUBED

2 CUPS GRATED MILD CHEDDAR CHEESE

1 CUP COOKED, CUBED HAM

¼ CUP CHOPPED GREEN BELL PEPPER

½ CUP FINELY CHOPPED ONION

6 EGGS

3 CUPS MILK (WHOLE, 2%, OR SKIM)

Mix bread, cheese, ham, bell pepper, and onion; spread in a 13x9x2-inch baking dish treated with nonstick spray. Whisk eggs and milk and pour over top. Cover dish with foil and freeze.

To prepare for serving, thaw dish and bake uncovered in a preheated 375°F oven for 45 minutes.

Summary of processes: Trim crusts from bread. Cut bread and ham into cubes; grate 2 cups mild cheddar cheese; chop ¼ cup green bell pepper and ½ cup onion
Freeze in: 13x9x2-inch baking dish
Serve with: Hot Spiced Fruit (page 149)
Note: This dish is good with 6 slices cooked, crumbled bacon instead of ham. You can also make this dish the night before, refrigerate it, then bake and serve it the next morning. It's nice for company brunch.

Makes 8 to 10 servings

Linguine à la Anne

1 12-OUNCE PACKAGE LINGUINE	1⅓ CUPS CHICKEN BROTH
2 TABLESPOONS MARGARINE	4 CUPS COOKED, CUBED HAM
2 TABLESPOONS ALL-PURPOSE FLOUR	½ CUP GRATED ROMANO CHEESE
½ TEASPOON SALT	1 SLICED RED BELL PEPPER
1 12-OUNCE CAN EVAPORATED SKIM MILK	1 SLICED GREEN BELL PEPPER
	1 TABLESPOON VEGETABLE OIL
1 4-OUNCE CAN MUSHROOM STEMS AND PIECES (RESERVE LIQUID)	1 CUP SEASONED CROUTONS*

Cook linguine in a large pot according to package directions, drain, and return to pot. While linguine cooks, melt margarine in a medium saucepan over low heat. Stir in flour and salt, adding evaporated milk. Bring to a boil, stirring constantly. Boil and stir 1 minute. Add reserved liquid from mushrooms and the chicken broth. Cook over medium heat, stirring constantly, until the sauce is bubbly and slightly thickened, about 10 minutes.

Add 2 cups of the sauce and drained mushrooms to the linguine and toss until well mixed. Spoon linguine mixture into a 13x9x2-inch baking dish, pressing it up the sides to leave a slight hollow in center of dish.

Toss ham in remaining sauce; spread it in the center of the linguine. Sprinkle with Romano cheese; cover with foil and freeze dish. Sauté red and green bell peppers in vegetable oil until soft, about 8 minutes; allow to cool. Put peppers in 1-quart freezer bag; attach this bag and croutons in a 1-quart freezer bag to the dish.

To prepare for serving, thaw dish, peppers, and croutons. Bake dish uncovered in a preheated 400°F oven for 20 minutes. Before serving, sprinkle croutons around edge of casserole. Reheat sautéed red and green bell peppers and mound them in the center.

Summary of processes: Cut ham into cubes; slice 1 red bell pepper and 1 green bell pepper

Freeze in: 13x9x2-inch baking dish; 2 1-quart bags

Serve with: Cooked zucchini, Orange Spiced Tea (page 143)

Note: Great for company that includes children.

Makes 8 servings

Calzones

2 LOAVES FROZEN BREAD DOUGH (ITALIAN, FRENCH, PIZZA, OR WHITE)

6 OUNCES GRATED MOZZARELLA CHEESE

5 CUPS SPAGHETTI SAUCE

Thaw two loaves of bread dough. Divide each loaf into 5 parts. One at a time, roll each dough piece on a floured board or stretch with your hands, making 10 7-inch squares. Fold each dough square over a pinch of cheese to form a turnover, and pinch edges to seal.

Place each turnover in a small sandwich bag. Put 5 turnovers in a 1-gallon freezer bag. Divide sauce in half and store in 2 1-quart freezer bags; enclose each bag of sauce in a bag of Calzones. Do the same with the remaining 5 turnovers.

To prepare for serving, thaw sauce; heat in a medium-size pot 10 to 15 minutes until bubbly. At the same time, take frozen turnovers out of bags and place them about 2 inches apart on a baking sheet sprayed with a nonstick spray. Preheat oven to 350°F. Bake for about 20 minutes. Turnovers will be golden brown when done. Ladle sauce on top of turnovers and serve.

Freeze in: 2 1-gallon bags; 2 1-quart bags; 10 sandwich bags
Serve with: Tossed salad with Italian dressing
Note: All ages love these! They're convenient, since you can bake only as many as needed at a time. Reheat for lunches.

Makes 10 servings

Mexican Stroganoff

2 POUNDS ROUND STEAK

1 CUP FINELY CHOPPED ONION

2 TEASPOONS MINCED GARLIC (2 CLOVES)

2 TABLESPOONS VEGETABLE OIL

1 CUP RED WINE

½ CUP WATER

½ CUP CHILI SAUCE

1 TABLESPOON PAPRIKA

1 TABLESPOON CHILI POWDER

2 TEASPOONS SEASONED SALT

1 TEASPOON SOY SAUCE

1 8-OUNCE CAN MUSHROOM STEMS AND PIECES, DRAINED

1 8-OUNCE CARTON SOUR CREAM OR PLAIN, LOW-FAT YOGURT*

3 TABLESPOONS ALL-PURPOSE FLOUR*

1 12-OUNCE PACKAGE WIDE EGG NOODLES*

Cut steak into bite-size pieces. Cook and stir steak, onion, and garlic in oil in a large saucepan over medium heat until brown, about 10 minutes. Drain oil. Stir in wine, water, chili sauce, paprika, chili powder, seasoned salt, soy sauce, and mushrooms. Bring to a boil; reduce heat. Cover and simmer 1 hour until meat is tender. Cool and store in freezer container.

To prepare for serving, thaw meat mixture and heat in saucepan until bubbly. Cook egg noodles according to package directions. Stir sour cream or plain low-fat yogurt and flour together; add to steak mixture. Heat to a boil, stirring constantly. Reduce heat; simmer and stir about 1 minute. Serve stroganoff over noodles.

Summary of processes: Cut steak in bite-size pieces; chop 1 cup onion; mince 2 cloves garlic
Freeze in: 6-cup container
Serve with: Tomatoes stuffed with guacamole, corn on the cob

Makes 6 to 8 servings

Balkan Meatballs

1 EGG	1 TABLESPOON MINCED ONION
¼ CUP MILK (WHOLE, 2%, OR SKIM)	1 8-OUNCE PACKAGE WIDE EGG
⅓ CUP CRUSHED SEASONED CROUTONS	NOODLES*
¾ TEASPOON SALT	
¾ TEASPOON SUGAR	*White Sauce*
¼ TEASPOON GROUND GINGER	2 TABLESPOONS MARGARINE*
¼ TEASPOON GROUND NUTMEG	¼ CUP ALL-PURPOSE FLOUR*
¼ TEASPOON GROUND ALLSPICE	2 CUPS MILK (WHOLE, 2%, OR SKIM)*
1 POUND LEAN GROUND BEEF	PARSLEY FOR GARNISH*
½ POUND GROUND TURKEY	

In a medium-size mixing bowl, beat egg with milk. Mix in the crushed croutons, salt, sugar, and spices. Add ground beef, ground turkey, and onion; mix thoroughly. Preheat oven to broil and/or 550°F. Shape meat mixture into meatballs the size of walnuts. Place meatballs on a rimmed cookie sheet; broil until lightly browned, about 5 minutes. Cool; put meatballs in a 1-gallon bag, and freeze them.

To prepare for serving, thaw meatballs. Cook noodles according to package directions. At the same time, make White Sauce in a large skillet. Melt margarine over low heat. Add flour, stirring constantly until mixture is smooth and bubbly. Gradually stir in milk. Heat to boiling over medium heat, stirring constantly. Boil and stir 1 minute until thick and smooth.

Add meatballs to sauce. Bring to a boil; reduce heat. Cover pan; simmer 15 minutes, stirring occasionally. Serve meatballs and sauce over wide egg noodles. Chop parsley; sprinkle over top.

Summary of processes: Crush ⅓ cup seasoned crouton crumbs
Freeze in: 1-gallon bag
Serve with: Cooked, fresh broccoli, cole slaw

Makes 4 servings

Marinated Flank Steak

Marinade
½ CUP VEGETABLE OIL
¼ CUP SOY SAUCE
¼ CUP SHERRY

2 TEASPOONS WORCESTERSHIRE SAUCE
½ TEASPOON GROUND GINGER
1 TEASPOON MINCED GARLIC (1 CLOVE)
1⅓ POUNDS FLANK STEAK

Mix first six ingredients for Marinade. Put flank steak in a freezer bag, pour marinade over it, seal bag, and freeze.

To prepare for serving, thaw flank steak, remove from marinade, and barbecue 8 to 10 minutes per side; or set oven control to broil and/or 550°F. Broil steak 6 inches from heat until brown, turning once, about 6 minutes on one side and 4 minutes on the other. Cut steak across grain at slanted angle into thin slices.

Summary of processes: Mince 1 clove garlic
Freeze in: 1-gallon bag
Serve with: Twice-Baked Potatoes Deluxe, page 150), cooked zucchini

Makes 4 servings

Chili Hamburgers

1 POUND LEAN GROUND BEEF OR TURKEY	1 TABLESPOON CHILI POWDER
	1 TABLESPOON CHILI SAUCE
2 TABLESPOONS FINELY CHOPPED GREEN BELL PEPPER	¼ TEASPOON BLACK PEPPER
	½ TEASPOON SALT
1 TABLESPOON MINCED ONION	4 HAMBURGER BUNS*

Thoroughly mix all ingredients except hamburger buns. Shape into 4 hamburger patties. Freeze in a large freezer bag, with waxed paper between each one.

To prepare for serving, thaw patties and hamburger buns. Grill or fry patties to desired pinkness in center. Serve on warmed hamburger buns.

Summary of processes: Chop 2 tablespoons green bell pepper
Freeze in: 1-gallon bag
Serve with: French fries or baked beans, Jiffy Salad (page 147)

Makes 4 servings

❑

CHAPTER 3

The Sprint: A Low-Fat Two-Week Entrée Plan

❑

GROCERY SHOPPING AND STAPLES LISTS

An asterisk (*) after an item indicates that it should be stored until you cook the dish with which it will be served. For example, the corn tortillas and salsa will not be used until the day you serve Chili Verde. Mark those items with an X as a reminder that you will need them for an entrée.

When entrées require perishable foods to be refrigerated until served, you may want to prepare those dishes right away or buy the food the week you plan to make the dish. For example, fresh mushrooms would spoil by the end of a month.

For the low-fat entrée plan, you will need these food items as well as the ones in the staples list that follows.

Grocery Shopping List

Canned Goods

    1 16-ounce can corn
    1 4-ounce can diced green chilies
    1 16-ounce can cut green beans
    1 8-ounce bottle lemon juice (½ cup)
    1 11-ounce can mandarin orange sections*

THE SPRINT:
A LOW-FAT TWO-WEEK ENTRÉE PLAN

SUN.	MON.	TUES.	WED.	THURS.	FRI.	SAT.
1 Eat Out Cooking Day!	2 Hearty Hamburger Tomato Stew	3 Chinese Chicken Morsels	4 Veggie Pizza	5 Grilled Fish	6 Chicken Spaghetti	7 Mandarin Orange Chicken
8 Vegetable Lasagna	9 Stove-Top Barbecued Chicken	10 Split Pea Soup	11 Blackened Chicken Breast	12 Chicken Cacciatore	13 Pizza Roll-Ups	14 Savory Beef
15 Chili Verde	16	17	18	19	20	21
22	23	24	25	26	27	28
29	30	31				

1 8-ounce can mushroom stems and pieces
1 3-ounce can sliced ripe olives
1 2-ounce jar pimientos
1 11½-ounce jar salsa*
1 46-ounce can tomato juice (low-sodium)
1 6-ounce can tomato paste
5 28-ounce cans Italian-style or plain crushed tomatoes in puree

Grains, Noodles, and Rice
1 8-ounce package lasagna
1 8-ounce package dry pinto beans
1 16-ounce package regular rice (1 cup)*
6 sandwich rolls*
1 12-ounce package spaghetti
1 packet dry spaghetti-sauce seasoning mix
1 8-ounce package wide egg noodles
1 16-ounce package spinach or wide egg noodles
1 12-ounce package dry, green split peas
1 dozen corn tortillas*

Frozen Foods
1¼ pounds frozen fish fillets (halibut, swordfish, or orange roughy)*
2 loaves frozen French, Italian, or all-purpose bread dough or Dawn's
French Bread (page 138)
1 6-ounce can frozen orange-juice concentrate

Dairy Products
8 ounces low-fat cheddar cheese
4 ounces reduced-fat Monterey Jack cheese
15 ounces part-skim mozzarella cheese
16 ounces low-fat ricotta cheese

Meat and Poultry
2 pounds chicken pieces
7 pounds boneless, skinless chicken breasts
2 pounds lean ground beef or turkey
2 pounds beef round tip steak
½ pound cooked turkey ham

Produce
3 green bell peppers
1 small red bell pepper (opt.)

2 medium stalks fresh broccoli
5 carrots (2¾ cups sliced)
1 bunch celery
4 cloves garlic
1¾ pounds fresh mushrooms (8 cups sliced)
1 bunch green onions
3 pounds white or yellow onions (6 medium)
1 bunch fresh parsley
5 or 6 new potatoes
1 medium zucchini

Staples List

Make sure you have the following staples on hand; add those you don't have to your shopping list.

basil leaves, dried
bay leaf
beef bouillon cubes (2)
brown sugar
catsup (⅓ cup)
celery seed
chicken bouillon cubes (6)
chili powder
cloves, ground
cumin, ground
Dijon mustard (¼ cup)
dill weed
dry mustard
flour, all-purpose
garlic powder
garlic salt
ginger, ground
Italian herb seasoning
light mayonnaise
low-fat margarine
nonstick spray
olive oil
onion powder
oregano leaves, dried
paprika
Parmesan cheese

pepper: cayenne, white, freshly ground black, and regular black
salt
soy sauce (¾ cup)
sugar
thyme leaves, dried
vegetable oil (about ½ cup)
white vinegar
Worcestershire sauce (about 3 tablespoons)

FREEZER CONTAINERS

The following list of freezer containers or flat baking dishes will be needed for the entrées in the two-week cycle. They're not the only containers in which you could freeze these foods, but the list gives you an idea of the size and number of containers you'll need.

1 Empty Spice Jar or Small Container
    Blackened Chicken

5 1-Gallon Freezer Bags
    Pizza Roll-Ups, 4; Chinese Chicken Morsels

8 1-Quart Freezer Bags
    Pizza Roll-Ups, 4; Grilled Fish; Blackened Chicken; Chicken Spaghetti; Chili Verde

Heavy Aluminum Foil
    Veggie Pizza; Vegetable Lasagna

1 12-Inch Pizza Pan or 10-Inch Pie Plate
    Veggie Pizza

2 4-Cup Freezer Containers
    Stove-Top Barbecued Chicken; Mandarin Orange Chicken

1 5-Cup Freezer Container
    Chili Verde

1 6-Cup Freezer Container
    Split Pea Soup

2 8-cup Freezer Containers
> Savory Beef; Chicken Cacciatore

2 16-cup Freezer Containers
> Hearty Hamburger Tomato Stew; Chicken Spaghetti

1 13x9x2-Inch Baking Dish
> Vegetable Lasagna

THE DAY BEFORE COOKING DAY

1. Freeze fish fillets, sandwich rolls, and 1½ pounds boneless, skinless chicken breasts for Blackened Chicken Breasts.
2. Use kitchen scissors or knife to cut 2 pounds raw, boneless chicken breasts into 1-inch cubes for Mandarin Orange Chicken and Chinese Chicken Morsels; refrigerate until needed.
3. In a large skillet, sauté remaining 3½ pounds boneless, skinless chicken breasts in a small amount of water until no longer pink in the center, about 25 minutes. Use kitchen scissors or knife to cut cooled chicken into 1-inch cubes. Store chicken in the refrigerator.
4. Set out appliances, bowls, canned goods, dry ingredients, freezer containers, and recipes.
5. Thaw 2 loaves of frozen bread dough in refrigerator overnight.
6. Rinse green split peas and soak them covered with cold water overnight. Do the same for pinto beans.

COOKING DAY ASSEMBLY ORDER

Make sure you've cleared the table and counters of unnecessary kitchenware to allow plenty of working room. It also helps to have fresh, damp washcloths and towels for wiping your hands and the cooking area. The day will go much more smoothly if you keep cleaning and organizing as you work.

Before you prepare a recipe, gather all the spices and ingredients in the assembly area to save time and steps. When you finish the recipe, remove unneeded items and wipe off the work space.

Slightly undercook regular rice and noodles (al dente) that will be frozen. When you reheat them, they will have a better consistency and won't turn mushy.

BEFORE ASSEMBLING DISHES

1. Put out 6-ounce can of frozen orange-juice concentrate to thaw.
2. Cook 2 pounds of ground beef or turkey until brown, about 15 minutes. Drain the oil and blot on a paper towel.
3. Perform all chopping, grating, and slicing tasks.

> Turkey ham: Cut into cubes.
> Beef: Slice round tip steak into strips about 2 inches long.
> Onions: Slice 2 onions; chop the rest.
> Green onions: Chop onion bulbs only; discard green tops.
> Broccoli: Chop fine 2 florets with small amount of stalks.
> Carrots: Slice 2¾ cups.
> Celery: Chop 1⅓ cups and slice 3 stalks, storing them in separate small bags.
> Garlic: Mince 4 cloves.
> Mushrooms: Slice all (8 cups).
> Parsley: Chop the whole bunch.
> Green bell peppers: Chop 2, slice half of the other into thin strips.
> Red bell pepper: Chop ½ cup.
> Zucchini: Chop 1 cup.
> Mozzarella, cheddar, and Monterey Jack cheeses: Grate all; put in separate bags.

4. Treat baking dishes and pie or pizza pans you will need with nonstick spray (check list of freezer containers on pages 35–36).
5. As you assemble each group of the following entrées, allow them to cool if necessary, put them in storage containers, and freeze.

Assemble Group 1 Entrées

1. Combine ingredients for Italian Tomato Sauce and start it simmering.
2. Assemble and bake Veggie Pizza.
3. Roll out dough for Pizza Roll-Ups. Assemble and bake them.
4. Mix ingredients for Hearty Hamburger Tomato Stew and start it simmering.
5. As soon as these dishes are completed and have cooled, label each one and freeze.

Assemble Group 2 Entrées

1. Cook lasagna and broccoli for Vegetable Lasagna and then finish assembling it.
2. Make marinade for Grilled Fish.
3. Label and freeze these dishes.

Assemble Group 3 Entrées

1. Assemble and start cooking Split Pea Soup and Chili Verde.
2. Complete Savory Beef in a skillet. Allow to cool, label and freeze.

Assemble Group 4 Entrées

1. Make Stove-Top Barbecued Chicken in one large skillet or pan with lid and Chicken Cacciatore in another.
2. While these are simmering, assemble Chinese Chicken Morsels.
3. Mix spices for Blackened Chicken Breasts.
4. Prepare Mandarin Orange Chicken.
5. Assemble Chicken Spaghetti, cooking noodles while chicken and tomato sauce are simmering.
6. Complete Split Pea Soup and Chili Verde; allow to cool.
7. Label and freeze this last batch of dishes.

Take a minute to enjoy looking into your freezer at all the food you've prepared!

RECIPES FOR THE LOW-FAT ENTRÉE PLAN

Each recipe offers complete instructions on how to prepare the dish. Food items with an asterisk (*) won't be prepared until you serve the entrée. For recipes calling for oven baking, preheat oven for about 10 minutes.

"Summary of processes" gives a quick overview of foods that need to be chopped, diced, grated, or sliced. "Freeze in" tells what bags and containers will be needed to freeze each entrée. "Serve with" offers suggestions of foods to accompany the meal. Some of the recipes for those foods are included in Chapter 8; page numbers are indicated for easy reference. "Note" includes special instructions on how the entrée can be used in other ways.

Italian Tomato Sauce

3 28-OUNCE CANS ITALIAN-STYLE OR PLAIN CRUSHED TOMATOES IN PUREE

3 TABLESPOONS SUGAR

3 TABLESPOONS ITALIAN HERB SEASONING

6 TABLESPOONS CHOPPED, FRESH PARSLEY

3 TABLESPOONS DRIED BASIL LEAVES

3 TEASPOONS GARLIC SALT

1½ TEASPOONS PEPPER

Mix all the ingredients in a heavy, large pot. Bring to a boil; reduce heat. Simmer 15 minutes, stirring occasionally. Save 3½ cups sauce for Vegetable Lasagna and 2 cups for Veggie Pizza. Divide remaining sauce into 4 1-cup portions, and put in 4 1-quart bags for Pizza Roll-Ups.

Summary of Processes: Chop 6 tablespoons parsley
Freeze in: 4 1-quart bags

Makes 9½ cups

Veggie Pizza

¼ CUP CHOPPED ONION	½ CUP GRATED PART-SKIM
¼ CUP CHOPPED RED BELL PEPPER	MOZZARELLA CHEESE
(OPT.)	1 LOAF FROZEN FRENCH, PIZZA,
¼ CUP CHOPPED GREEN BELL PEPPER	ITALIAN, OR ALL-PURPOSE BREAD
1 CUP CHOPPED ZUCCHINI	DOUGH OR DAWN'S FRENCH
1 CUP SLICED FRESH MUSHROOMS	BREAD (PAGE 138)
1 TABLESPOON VEGETABLE OIL	2 CUPS ITALIAN TOMATO SAUCE

Preheat oven to 400°F. Sauté vegetables in oil until transparent, about 10 minutes. Drain well and allow to cool. Stir in cheese. Roll dough into a ½-inch-thick circle. Put dough on a 12-inch pizza pan or 10-inch pie plate. Spread Italian Tomato Sauce on pizza. Spoon vegetable mixture over sauce. Bake for 20 minutes. Cool, cover pizza with heavy aluminum foil, and freeze.

To prepare for serving, thaw and then heat pizza in a preheated 400°F oven for about 20 minutes.

Summary of processes: Chop ¼ cup onion, ¼ cup red bell pepper, ¼ cup green bell pepper, 1 cup zucchini; slice 1 cup fresh mushrooms; grate ½ cup part-skim mozzarella cheese
Freeze in: 12-inch pizza pan or 10-inch pie pan; heavy aluminum foil
Serve with: Lemon gelatin with pears
Note: A tasty addition to this pizza is ½ pound browned turkey sausage, 1 teaspoon parsley, 1 teaspoon dried basil leaves, 1 teaspoon dried oregano leaves, and ½ teaspoon salt.

Makes 6 servings

Pizza Roll-Ups

1 LOAF FROZEN FRENCH, ITALIAN OR
   ALL-PURPOSE BREAD DOUGH, OR
   DAWN'S FRENCH BREAD
   (PAGE 138)
1 POUND LEAN GROUND BEEF OR
   TURKEY (2½ CUPS BROWNED)
1 TEASPOON SALT

½ TEASPOON PEPPER
2 CUPS GRATED PART-SKIM
   MOZZARELLA CHEESE
1 TEASPOON ITALIAN SEASONING
1 TABLESPOON CHOPPED FRESH
   PARSLEY

4 CUPS ITALIAN TOMATO SAUCE*

Thaw dough; roll it into a 14x24-inch rectangle about ¼-inch thick. Cook ground beef or turkey until brown, about 10 minutes. Drain fat. Stir in remaining ingredients except Italian Tomato Sauce. Spoon filling evenly onto dough, slightly pressing filling into dough.

Roll dough lengthwise like a jelly roll and cut into 24 1-inch slices. Treat 2 rimmed cookie sheets with nonstick spray; lay slices on sheets about an inch apart. Preheat oven to 400°F. Let Roll-Ups sit for 10 minutes. Bake for 20 to 25 minutes or until golden brown. Cool and freeze in 4 1-gallon bags, 6 per bag. Slip a 1-quart bag with 1 cup sauce into each bag of Pizza Roll-Ups.

To prepare, thaw Roll-Ups and warm them in a preheated 400°F oven for 10 minutes. Or put them frozen in the microwave; heat on high for about 2 minutes. Serve with warmed Italian Tomato Sauce.

> *Summary of processes:* Chop 1 tablespoon parsley; grate 2 cups part-skim mozzarella cheese
> *Freeze in:* 4 1-gallon bags, Roll-Ups; 4 1-quart bags, Italian Tomato Sauce
> Serve with: Tossed green salad
> *Note:* These Roll-Ups are super for picnics or nights when the family must eat in shifts. They can be eaten warm or cold. They're also a favorite with kids and an easy snack.

Makes 24 servings

Hearty Hamburger Tomato Stew

1 POUND LEAN GROUND BEEF OR
    TURKEY (2½ CUPS BROWNED)

1¼ CUPS CHOPPED ONION

2 CUPS PEELED AND SLICED CARROTS

1 CUP CHOPPED GREEN BELL PEPPER

1 CUP SLICED FRESH MUSHROOMS

1 16-OUNCE CAN CUT GREEN BEANS,
    DRAINED

1 16-OUNCE CAN CORN, DRAINED

3 STALKS SLICED CELERY

1 46-OUNCE CAN TOMATO JUICE (LOW-
    SODIUM)

2 TEASPOONS SUGAR

1 TEASPOON CELERY SEED

SALT AND PEPPER TO TASTE

Cook ground beef or turkey in a large saucepan until brown, about 10 to 15 minutes. Drain the fat and mix in remaining ingredients. Bring to a boil; reduce heat. Simmer covered 30 minutes, stirring occasionally. Cool and freeze.

To prepare for serving, thaw stew. Then bring to a boil; reduce heat; simmer 10 minutes.

Summary of processes: Chop 1¼ cups onion and 1 cup green bell pepper; peel and slice 2 cups carrots, 1 cup fresh mushrooms, 3 stalks celery
Freeze in: 16-cup container
Serve with: Cornbread or wheat crackers

Makes 8 servings

Vegetable Lasagna

1 8-OUNCE PACKAGE LASAGNA

2 STALKS FINELY CHOPPED BROCCOLI
    FLORETS

1 16-OUNCE CARTON LOW-FAT RICOTTA
    CHEESE

1 CUP GRATED PART-SKIM MOZZARELLA
    CHEESE

1 8-OUNCE CAN MUSHROOM STEMS AND
    PIECES, DRAINED

2 CHOPPED GREEN ONION BULBS
    (WITHOUT GREENS)

2 TEASPOONS DRIED BASIL LEAVES

1½ TEASPOONS CRUMBLED DRIED
    OREGANO LEAVES

¼ CUP FINELY CHOPPED FRESH
    PARSLEY

DASH OF FRESHLY GROUND BLACK
    PEPPER

3½ CUPS ITALIAN TOMATO SAUCE

Boil lasagna 10 minutes or until al dente, stirring occasionally to prevent noodles from sticking. Drain noodles, rinse in cold water, and then lay them next to each other on waxed paper to dry. Cook broccoli 5 minutes in boiling water.

Combine cheeses, remaining vegetables, herbs, and pepper in a medium bowl. In a 13x9x2-inch dish, layer lasagna noodles, spread with half the cheese mixture, and half the tomato sauce. Repeat process, topping with noodles and covering with sauce. Wrap dish with foil and freeze.

To prepare for serving, thaw dish. Preheat oven to 350°F. Bake covered for 20 minutes. Remove foil, and bake 15 to 20 minutes more until heated through.

Summary of processes: Grate 1 cup part-skim mozzarella cheese; chop 2 small broccoli stalks, 2 green onion bulbs, ¼ cup parsley

Freeze in: 13x9x2-inch baking dish

Serve with: Fresh fruit salad, bread sticks

Note: For an alternate way to prepare this entrée, use large shell pasta. Cook pasta as directed on package until al dente. Stuff each shell with cheese mixture. Freeze stuffed shells on a rimmed baking sheet. When they're hard, transfer them to a freezer bag. Freeze sauce in a separate bag taped to pasta bag. Thaw number of shells and amount of sauce desired. Warm them in a preheated 350°F oven about 20 minutes. Serve shells with warmed sauce poured over them.

Makes 12 servings

Grilled Fish

1¼ POUNDS FROZEN FISH FILLETS
(HALIBUT, SWORDFISH, OR
ORANGE ROUGHY)*
5 TO 6 NEW POTATOES*

Marinade
½ CUP SOY SAUCE (LOW-SODIUM)
¼ CUP WATER
¼ CHICKEN BOUILLON CUBE
2 TABLESPOONS OLIVE OIL
1 TABLESPOON BROWN SUGAR
2 TEASPOONS MINCED GARLIC
(2 CLOVES)
½ TEASPOON GROUND GINGER

Freeze fish fillets and store new potatoes until you're ready to serve them. Whisk remaining ingredients in a small bowl to make Marinade. Freeze in a plastic bag taped to fish-fillet package.

To prepare for serving, thaw Marinade and fish fillets. Marinate fish 30 minutes. Prepare new potatoes. Heat 1 cup salted water to a boil; add potatoes. Cover, heat until boiling; then reduce heat. Simmer tightly covered until tender, 30 to 35 minutes; drain.

At the same time, remove fish from the marinade. Set oven control to broil and/or 550°F. Broil or grill fish for 10 minutes per inch of thickness or until fish flakes easily with a fork. Baste frequently with Marinade while cooking. If fish is more than 1-inch thick, turn once during cooking.

Summary of processes: Mince 2 garlic cloves
Freeze in: 1-quart bag taped to fish fillet package
Serve with: Tossed green salad

Makes 4 servings

Split Pea Soup

1 12-OUNCE PACKAGE DRY, GREEN SPLIT PEAS	**⅛ TEASPOON FRESHLY GROUND PEPPER**
3 CUPS WATER	**⅓ CUP CHOPPED CELERY**
½ POUND COOKED, CUBED TURKEY HAM	**¾ CUP PEELED AND SLICED CARROTS**
¾ TEASPOON ONION POWDER	**1 CUP CHOPPED ONION**
⅛ TEASPOON DRIED THYME LEAVES	**1 BAY LEAF**
	SALT TO TASTE

Rinse split peas, soak them in cold water overnight; drain. Put peas with remaining ingredients in a large pot. Bring to a boil; reduce heat. Stirring occasionally, simmer about 2 hours until peas are tender and turn pasty. Cool and freeze.

To serve, thaw soup and simmer until warmed through. If peas are too condensed, add water to make consistency of thick soup.

Summary of processes: Soak split peas in water overnight; cut ham into cubes; peel and slice ¾ cup carrots; chop 1 cup onion, ⅓ cup celery
Freeze in: 6-cup container
Serve with: Orange slices or canned peaches, cornbread

Makes 6 servings

Chili Verde

1 8-OUNCE PACKAGE DRY PINTO BEANS (1¼ CUPS)

1 POUND BONELESS, SKINLESS CHICKEN BREASTS

1 4-OUNCE CAN CHOPPED GREEN CHILIES

1 TEASPOON GROUND CUMIN

¾ TEASPOON DRIED OREGANO LEAVES

⅛ TEASPOON GROUND CLOVES

⅛ TEASPOON CAYENNE PEPPER

3 CUPS WATER

3 CHICKEN BOUILLON CUBES

1 TEASPOON MINCED GARLIC (1 CLOVE)

1 TEASPOON SALT

⅔ CUP FINELY CHOPPED ONION

1 CUP GRATED LOW-FAT MONTEREY JACK CHEESE*

1 DOZEN CORN TORTILLAS*

1 11½-OUNCE JAR SALSA*

Rinse pinto beans, soak them in cold water overnight, then drain them. Cut chicken into 1-inch cubes; cook in a small amount of water or vegetable oil until no longer pink, about 15 minutes. Combine chicken with chilies and seasonings; refrigerate until needed. At the same time, combine beans, water, bouillon cubes, garlic, salt, and onion in a large pot; bring to a boil.

Reduce heat and simmer until beans are soft, about 1 hour. Add more water if necessary.

Combine chicken and spices with beans; simmer 10 more minutes. Cool and freeze. Grate cheese, put it in a 1-quart bag, and attach it to the freezer container with the chili.

To serve, thaw chili and cheese. Simmer chili 30 minutes, stirring occasionally. Top chili with salsa and grated cheese; serve on warmed corn tortillas.

Summary of processes: Soak ½ pound pinto beans overnight; cut 1 pound boneless chicken into 1-inch cubes; chop ⅔ cup onion; grate 1 cup low-fat Monterey Jack cheese
Freeze in: 5-cup container; 1-quart bag
Serve with: Tossed green salad

Makes 5 servings

Savory Beef

2 POUNDS BEEF ROUND TIP STEAK

FRESHLY GROUND BLACK PEPPER TO
    TASTE

1 CUP SLICED FRESH MUSHROOMS

1 SLICED ONION

3 TABLESPOONS VEGETABLE OIL

3 TABLESPOONS ALL-PURPOSE FLOUR

2 CUPS WATER

2 BEEF BOUILLON CUBES

2 TABLESPOONS TOMATO PASTE

1 TEASPOON DRY MUSTARD

¼ TEASPOON DRIED OREGANO LEAVES

¼ TEASPOON DILL WEED

2 TABLESPOONS WORCESTERSHIRE
    SAUCE

1 8-OUNCE PACKAGE WIDE EGG
    NOODLES*

Cut beef into thin strips about 2 inches long. Sprinkle beef with pepper and set meat aside in a cool place. In a heavy skillet, sauté mushrooms and onions in oil until golden, about 10 to 15 minutes. Remove them from skillet. Put meat in same skillet; cook and stir steak quickly on all sides until it's brown but still rare in the center, about 7 minutes. Remove meat and set aside.

Blend flour into the drippings in skillet, gradually adding water and beef bouillon. Bring to a boil. Stir constantly until smooth and slightly thick. Mix in tomato paste, dry mustard, oregano, dill weed, and Worcestershire sauce. Stir meat, mushrooms, and onions into sauce. Cool meat mixture and freeze.

To prepare for serving, thaw beef. Prepare noodles according to package directions. Heat beef in a saucepan over medium heat, stirring constantly until it's bubbly. Serve meat over noodles.

Summary of processes: Slice 1 cup fresh mushrooms and 1 onion
Freeze in: 8-cup container
Serve with: French-cut green beans
Note: Use any leftover beef for sandwiches

Makes 6 servings

Stove-Top Barbequed Chicken

1 TEASPOON VEGETABLE OIL

1 CUP FINELY CHOPPED ONION

⅓ CUP CATSUP

⅓ CUP WATER

4 TEASPOONS WHITE VINEGAR

4 TEASPOONS BROWN SUGAR

1½ TEASPOONS WORCESTERSHIRE
SAUCE

½ TEASPOON CHILI POWDER

¼ TEASPOON CRUSHED CELERY SEEDS

2 POUNDS SKINNED CHICKEN PIECES

1 16-OUNCE PACKAGE SPINACH OR
WIDE EGG NOODLES (USE HALF)*

Heat oil in a large, nonstick skillet; sauté onion until tender, about 5 to 10 minutes. Drain the oil. Stir in catsup, water, vinegar, brown sugar, Worcestershire sauce, chili powder, and celery seeds. Bring sauce to a boil. Add the chicken to the skillet, placing the side down that has the skin removed; spoon sauce over the pieces. Bring to a boil; reduce heat. Cover and simmer 30 minutes. Turn chicken pieces, and simmer covered for about 20 minutes more or until chicken is cooked through. Cool and freeze chicken and sauce.

To prepare for serving, thaw chicken and sauce; put in a large skillet, and cook over medium heat, stirring constantly until bubbly, about 20 to 25 minutes. Cook half package of spinach or egg noodles according to directions; serve chicken over noodles.

Summary of processes: Chop 1 cup onion
Freeze in: 4-cup container
Serve with: Corn on the cob, Low-Calorie Chocolate Cake (page 145)

Makes 4 servings

Chicken Cacciatore

1 POUND BONELESS, SKINLESS
CHICKEN BREASTS (2 CUPS
COOKED)

1 TABLESPOON VEGETABLE OIL

1 SLICED MEDIUM ONION

½ SLICED GREEN BELL PEPPER

2 CUPS SLICED FRESH MUSHROOMS

1 TEASPOON MINCED GARLIC (1 CLOVE)

1 28-OUNCE CAN ITALIAN-STYLE OR
PLAIN CRUSHED TOMATOES IN
PUREE

2 TABLESPOONS CHOPPED FRESH
PARSLEY

1 TEASPOON SALT

¼ TEASPOON PEPPER

2 TEASPOONS ITALIAN SEASONING

1 TEASPOON DRIED BASIL LEAVES

PARMESAN CHEESE*

1 16-OUNCE PACKAGE SPINACH OR
WIDE EGG NOODLES (USE HALF)*

Cut chicken into 1-inch cubes. In a large skillet, sauté chicken in vegetable oil until no longer pink in the center, about 15 minutes. Remove chicken from skillet and sauté onion, green bell pepper, mushrooms, and garlic until onion is transparent, about 10 minutes. Add chicken and remaining ingredients except Parmesan cheese and noodles to the skillet. Simmer 15 minutes. Allow sauce to cool, put in an 8-cup container, cover with foil and freeze.

To serve, thaw dish, and bake chicken in a preheated oven at 350°F for 35 minutes. Cook half package spinach or egg noodles according to directions. Serve chicken over noodles and sprinkle on Parmesan cheese.

Summary of processes: Cut 1 pound chicken into cubes; slice 1 medium onion, ½ green bell pepper, 2 cups fresh mushrooms; mince 1 clove garlic
Freeze in: 8-cup container
Serve with: Cooked baby carrots, Dawn's French Bread (page 138)

Makes 6 servings

Chinese Chicken Morsels

1 POUND BONELESS, SKINLESS CHICKEN BREASTS (2 CUPS)

Marinade
½ CUP LEMON JUICE
¼ CUP SOY SAUCE

¼ CUP DIJON MUSTARD
2 TEASPOONS VEGETABLE OIL
¼ TEASPOON CAYENNE PEPPER
1 CUP REGULAR, UNCOOKED RICE*

Cut chicken breasts (kitchen scissors work best) into 1-inch cubes. Mix lemon juice, soy sauce, mustard, oil, and pepper. Put Marinade and chicken cubes in a 1-gallon bag and store in the freezer.

To prepare for serving, thaw chicken and remove from Marinade. Warm Marinade in a small saucepan. Place cubes about an inch apart on broiler pan treated with nonstick spray. Broil 4 to 5 inches from heat for 7 minutes, brushing with Marinade once. Turn chicken cubes and broil another 4 minutes. Meanwhile, prepare rice according to package directions. Heat remaining Marinade and serve over rice.

Summary of processes: Cut chicken into 1-inch cubes
Freeze in: 1-gallon bag
Serve with: Sliced, fresh tomatoes or tossed salad, Spicy Pumpkin Muffins (page 142)
Note: For a luncheon alternative, toss sautéed or broiled chicken morsels with mixed

salad greens, shredded carrots, cherry tomatoes, chopped green bell pepper, sliced water chestnuts, and croutons. Use your favorite low-calorie dressing.

Makes 4 to 5 servings

Blackened Chicken Breasts

1½ **POUNDS BONELESS, SKINLESS CHICKEN BREASTS***
6 **SANDWICH ROLLS***
1 **TABLESPOON VEGETABLE OIL***
LOW-FAT MARGARINE OR LIGHT MAYONNAISE*
¼ **CUP MELTED LOW-FAT MARGARINE***

Spice Mix*
2 **TEASPOONS PAPRIKA**
1 **TEASPOON ONION POWDER**
1 **TEASPOON GARLIC POWDER**
¼ **TEASPOON CAYENNE PEPPER**
½ **TEASPOON WHITE PEPPER**
½ **TEASPOON BLACK PEPPER**
½ **TEASPOON SALT**
½ **TEASPOON DRIED THYME LEAVES**
½ **TEASPOON DRIED OREGANO LEAVES**

Freeze chicken and sandwich rolls until ready to serve. Mix spices; store in a covered container such as an empty spice jar, which you've labeled "Blackened Chicken Spices."

To serve, thaw rolls and chicken. Coat each piece of chicken with about 1 tablespoon spice mix. The mixture is hot and spicy, so adjust amount for taste of each person. Using a pastry brush, baste each piece of chicken with melted, low-fat margarine. Grill chicken, basting with low-fat margarine after turning once. Grill about 10 minutes or until no longer pink in the middle. Or cook chicken in a large, nonstick skillet in hot oil over medium heat. Cook, turning chicken once, until it's done, about 10 minutes. Serve on sandwich rolls spread with a little margarine or light mayonnaise.

Summary of processes: Mix spices
Freeze in: 1-quart bag
Serve with: Applesauce, carrot and celery strips
Note: Use spice mix on your favorite fish fillets

Makes 6 servings

Mandarin Orange Chicken

1 POUND BONELESS, SKINLESS
    CHICKEN BREASTS (2 CUPS)
1 TABLESPOON VEGETABLE OIL
2 CUPS SLICED, FRESH MUSHROOMS
2 TEASPOONS ALL-PURPOSE FLOUR
⅔ CUP WATER
1 6-OUNCE CAN FROZEN ORANGE-JUICE
    CONCENTRATE, THAWED

½ CUP THINLY SLICED GREEN ONION
    BULBS (WITHOUT GREENS)
2 CHICKEN BOUILLON CUBES
1 11-OUNCE CAN MANDARIN ORANGE
    SECTIONS, DRAINED*
1 CUP REGULAR, UNCOOKED RICE*

Cut chicken into 1-inch chunks with kitchen scissors or knife. Heat oil in large skillet; add chicken, and cook on medium high until browned on both sides, about 15 minutes. Remove and set aside chicken. In the same skillet, cook mushrooms over medium high, stirring constantly. Sprinkle flour over mushrooms, stirring quickly to combine. Gradually stir in water, orange-juice concentrate, green onions, and bouillon cubes. Stirring constantly, bring to a boil. Reduce heat, add chicken, and let simmer 3 to 4 minutes. Cool and freeze.

To serve, thaw chicken mixture, and cook rice according to package directions. Heat chicken mixture in a saucepan until bubbly, stir in drained orange segments and heat through. Combine with cooked rice and serve.

Summary of processes: Cut 1 pound chicken into chunks; slice 2 cups fresh mushrooms, ½ cup green onion bulbs
Freeze in: 4-cup container
Serve with: French-cut green beans, biscuits

Makes 4 servings

Chicken Spaghetti

1 12-OUNCE PACKAGE SPAGHETTI
    (SEMOLINA)
1½ POUNDS BONELESS, SKINLESS
    CHICKEN BREASTS (3 CUPS
    COOKED)
1 28-OUNCE CAN ITALIAN-STYLE OR
    PLAIN CRUSHED TOMATOES IN
    PUREE
1 2-OUNCE JAR PIMENTOS
1 CUP CHOPPED GREEN BELL PEPPER

1 CUP CHOPPED CELERY
1 CUP SLICED FRESH MUSHROOMS
1½ CUPS CHOPPED ONION
1 3-OUNCE CAN SLICED RIPE OLIVES
1 PACKET DRY SPAGHETTI SAUCE
    SEASONING
SALT AND PEPPER TO TASTE
2 CUPS GRATED LOW-FAT CHEDDAR
    CHEESE*

Cook spaghetti until al dente; drain. At the same time, cut chicken into 1-inch cubes; cook chicken in a small amount of water until no longer pink in the center, about 15 minutes. In a large pot, combine chicken with remaining ingredients except cheese. Bring mixture to a boil; reduce heat. Simmer for 15 minutes, stirring occasionally. Add cooked spaghetti to sauce. Cool and freeze in 16-cup container; tape 1-quart bag with cheese to container.

To prepare for serving, thaw cheese and spaghetti. Bake spaghetti in a preheated 325°F oven for 40 minutes. Top spaghetti with cheese; return spaghetti to oven for 5 minutes or until cheese melts.

Summary of processes: Cut 1½ pounds chicken into 1-inch cubes; chop 1 cup green bell pepper, 1 cup celery, and 1½ cups onion; slice 1 cup fresh mushrooms; grate 2 cups low-fat cheddar cheese
Freeze in: 16-cup container; 1-quart bag
Serve with: Tossed green salad, Cheesy-Herb Bread (page 135)

Makes 10 servings

❑

CHAPTER 4

The Shot Put:
A Two-Week Entrée Plan

❑

GROCERY SHOPPING AND STAPLES LISTS

An asterisk (*) after an item indicates it can be stored until you cook the dish with which it will be served. For example, the can of mandarin oranges will not be needed until the day you serve Country Captain. Mark those items with an X before you put them away as a reminder that you will need them for an entrée.

When entrées require perishable foods to be refrigerated until served, you may want to use those dishes right away or buy the food the week you plan to prepare the dish.

For this two-week entrée plan you will need these food items as well as the ones on the staples list that follows.

Grocery Shopping List

Canned Goods

   1 4-ounce can mushroom pieces and stems
   1 10¾-ounce can cream of mushroom soup
   5 14½-ounce cans stewed tomatoes
   1 14½-ounce can Mexican-style stewed tomatoes
   2 8-ounce cans tomato sauce
   1 15-ounce can tomato sauce

THE SHOT PUT:
A TWO-WEEK ENTRÉE PLAN

SUN.	MON.	TUES.	WED.	THURS.	FRI.	SAT.
				1 *Eat Out Cooking Day!*	2 *Herbed Chicken*	3 *Biscuit Beef Bake*
4 *French Stuffed Potatoes*	5 *Chicken Nuggets*	6 *Playoff Burgers*	7 *Farmer's Casserole*	8 *Poppy Turkey*	9 *Crab Shells*	10 *Country Captain*
11 *Denise's Black Beans*	12 *Spicy Garlic Chicken Pizza*	13 *London Broil*	14 *Mexican Chicken Lasagna*	15 *Sopa de Maíz*	16	17
18	19	20	21	22	23	24
25	26	27	28	29	30	31

½ cup salsa, medium or mild

5 15-ounce cans black beans

2 4-ounce cans chopped green chilies

1 12-ounce can evaporated milk or evaporated skim milk

Grains, Pasta, and Rice

2 5.7-ounce boxes of couscous* (or enough to serve 6)

1 16-ounce (12-inch) Italian bread shell (Boboli brand) or tube of pizza crust dough

32-ounce bag of rice*

2 10-ounce boxes uncooked lasagna noodles

8 ounces linguine

6 whole wheat buns or Kaiser rolls

12 jumbo pasta shells

Dry Ingredients and Seasonings

½ cup dried bread crumbs—Italian style

¼ cup slivered almonds

1 1¼-ounce package taco seasoning

1 10½-ounce bag of Fritos or corn chips*

Frozen Foods

1 16-ounce bag frozen corn

1 26-ounce bag frozen shredded hash brown potatoes

Dairy Products

2 sticks butter or margarine

1¼ cups grated Parmesan cheese

3 cups (12 ounces) grated Monterey Jack cheese

1 cup (4 ounces) Monterey Jack cheese with jalapeño peppers (also called hot pepper cheese)

2 ounces mozzarella cheese, grated

7 eggs

1 16-ounce container ricotta cheese

4½ cups milk

½ cup each grated Swiss and cheddar cheese

1 cup cottage cheese

1 8-ounce package light cream cheese

1 cup plain low-fat yogurt

1 12-ounce package Hungry Jack buttermilk biscuits*

1 cup sour cream (or plain low-fat yogurt)

Note: See Chapter 10 for ounce/cup equivalent measures.

Meat, Poultry, and Seafood

6 pounds boneless, skinless chicken breasts
5 to 6 pounds chicken pieces
2 pounds ground turkey
4 pounds lean ground beef
2 pounds London broil
⅓ pound fully cooked ham
1 pound smoked sausage links (e.g., Lit'l Smokies)
½ pound crabmeat or imitation crabmeat

Produce

5 to 6 large bunches green onions
11 cloves garlic
½ cup fresh parsley
¼ cup currants or raisins
4 medium yellow onions
1 tomato*
1 avocado*
4 large baking potatoes*
2 green bell peppers
1 bunch celery
1 lemon

Staples List

A-1 sauce
basil
bay leaves
black pepper
brown sugar
cayenne pepper
chicken bouillon cubes (4)
chili powder
cornstarch
cumin
curry powder
Dijon mustard
flour, all-purpose
ginger, ground
mace or nutmeg, ground
onion salt
oregano leaves, dried

THE DAY BEFORE COOKING DAY

1. Store the Hungry Jack buttermilk biscuits, rice, couscous, Fritos, 1 tomato, 1 avocado, 4 large baking potatoes, and linguine in the refrigerator or cupboard until the day you will be serving the corresponding entrée. Be sure to label each so you won't forget to use them for other dishes.
2. Bring 3 pounds boneless, skinless chicken breasts to boil in a large pot in at least 6 cups of water. Boil gently until chicken is tender and no longer pink in the center—about 15 minutes. Drain, reserving 3 cups chicken broth. Chop the cooked chicken. Refrigerate until ready to use on cooking day.
3. Set out appliances, canned goods, dry ingredients, freezer containers, and recipes.

COOKING DAY ASSEMBLY ORDER

Make sure you've cleared the table and counters of unnecessary kitchenware to allow plenty of working room. It also helps to have fresh, damp washcloths and towels for wiping your hands and the cooking area. The day will go a lot more smoothly if you clean and organize as you work.

Before you prepare a recipe, gather all the spices and ingredients in the assembly area to save time and steps. When you finish the recipe, remove unneeded items and wipe off the work space.

BEFORE ASSEMBLING DISHES

1. Perform all chopping, crushing, grating, and slicing tasks.
    Parsley: Chop ¼ cup.
    Celery: Chop 1½ cups.
    Green pepper: Chop 2 cups.
    Green onions: Slice 5 to 6 large bunches to make 2½ cups.
    Monterey Jack cheese with Jalepeño peppers: Grate 1 cup.
    Mozzarella cheese: Grate ½ cup.
    Swiss cheese: Grate ½ cup.
    Lemon zest: Grate 2 tablespoons.
    Boneless chicken breast: Cube 3 pounds (use kitchen scissors for best results).
    Ham: Cube 1 cup.
    Smoked sausage: Slice 1 pound.
    Onions: Chop 3¾ cups.
    Garlic: Mince 10 cloves.
2. Assemble Denise's Black Beans in a Crock-Pot

poppy seeds
salsa
salt
soy sauce
sugar
thyme leaves, dried
vegetable oil
white vinegar
Worcestershire sauce

FREEZER CONTAINERS

The following list of freezer containers or flat baking dishes will be needed for
this two-week entrée plan. They're not the only containers in which you ca
foods, but the list gives you an idea of the size and number of containers you'l

9 1-Gallon Freezer Bags

Chicken Nuggets; Spicy Garlic Chicken Pizza; Herbed Chicken; Cou
French Stuffed Potatoes; Poppy Turkey (2); Playoff Burgers; London

5 1-Quart Freezer Bags

Chicken Nuggets; Spicy Garlic Chicken Pizza (2); French Stuffed Pot
Burgers

2 13x9x2-Inch Baking Dishes

Mexican Chicken Lasagna; Farmer's Casserole

1 10-Inch Round Baking Dish

Crab Shells

1 5-Cup Container

Biscuit Beef Bake

1 6-Cup Container

Sopa de Maiz

1 10-Cup Container

Denise's Black Beans

Assemble Chicken Dishes

1. Assemble Chicken Nuggets.
2. Assemble Spicy Garlic Chicken.
3. While chicken is marinating in refrigerator, assemble Herbed Chicken.
4. Assemble Country Captain.
5. While Country Captain simmers, complete Spicy Garlic Chicken Pizza and freeze.
6. Assemble Mexican Chicken Lasagna.
7. Assemble Sopa de Maiz.
8. Label and freeze chicken dishes.

Assemble Beef and Ground Turkey Dishes

1. For the Biscuit Beef Bake and French Stuffed Potatoes, cook 2 pounds ground beef until brown, about 25 minutes. Drain the fat. Sauté the ½ cup chopped onion with 1 teaspoon minced garlic until transparent, about 10 minutes. Finish these dishes.
2. Assemble Poppy Turkey.
3. Assemble Playoff Burgers.
4. Make sauce for London Broil.
5. Label and freeze beef and ground turkey dishes.

Assemble Seafood and Miscellaneous Dishes

1. Assemble Crab Shells.
2. Assemble Farmer's Casserole.
3. Label and freeze these two dishes.
4. Cool Denise's Black Beans after they've cooked 8 hours. Label and freeze.

RECIPES FOR THE SHOT-PUT:
TWO-WEEK ENTRÉE PLAN

Each recipe offers complete instructions on how to prepare the dish. Food items with an asterisk (*) won't be prepared until you serve the entrée. For recipes calling for oven baking, preheat oven for about 10 minutes.

   "Summary of processes" gives a quick overview of foods that need to be chopped, diced, grated, or sliced. "Freeze in" tells what bags and containers will be needed to freeze each entrée. "Serve with" offers suggestions of foods to accompany the meal. Some of the recipes for those foods are included in Chapter 8; page numbers are indicated for easy reference. "Note" includes special instructions on how the entrée can be used in other ways.

Denise's Black Beans

1 POUND SMOKED SAUSAGE CUT INTO PIECES (E.G., LIT'L SMOKIES)

3 15-OUNCE CANS BLACK BEANS, DRAINED

1½ CUPS CHOPPED ONION

1½ CUPS CHOPPED GREEN BELL PEPPER

1½ CUPS CHOPPED CELERY

4 TEASPOONS MINCED GARLIC (4 CLOVES)

2 TEASPOONS DRIED THYME LEAVES

1½ TEASPOONS DRIED OREGANO LEAVES

1½ TEASPOONS PEPPER

¼ TEASPOON CAYENNE PEPPER

1 CHICKEN BOUILLON CUBE

5 BAY LEAVES

1 8-OUNCE CAN TOMATO SAUCE

1 CUP WATER

RICE (TO SERVE 8)*

Combine all ingredients, except rice, in a Crock-Pot. Cook on low for 8 hours. Remove bay leaves. Cool to room temperature and freeze.

When preparing to serve, heat to boiling and simmer 15 minutes. Serve over hot, cooked rice.

Summary of processes: Chop 1½ cups onion, 1½ cups green pepper, and 1½ cups celery; mince 4 cloves garlic

Serve with: Rice, Blueberry Peach Fruit Crisp (page 145)

Freeze in: 1 6-cup container

Makes 8 servings

Chicken Nuggets

2 POUNDS BONELESS, SKINLESS CHICKEN BREASTS

3 TABLESPOONS MARGARINE OR BUTTER, MELTED

2 TEASPOONS WORCESTERSHIRE SAUCE

½ CUP DRIED BREAD CRUMBS — ITALIAN STYLE

⅓ CUP GRATED PARMESAN CHEESE

Cut chicken into 1-inch pieces (kitchen shears work best). Combine chicken, melted margarine, and Worcestershire in a 1-quart freezer bag to make a marinade. Combine the bread crumbs and Parmesan cheese in a second freezer bag. Tape the two bags together. Label and freeze.

To prepare for serving, thaw and remove the chicken pieces from marinade. Shake them in the bread-crumb bag to coat, a few at a time. Preheat oven to 450°F. Arrange chicken on a greased cookie sheet. Bake for 7 to 9 minutes or until no longer pink in the center.

Summary of processes: Cut 2 pounds boneless, skinless chicken into 1-inch pieces
Freeze in: 1-gallon bag; 1-quart bag
Serve with: Chips and dips; green bean casserole; catsup or barbecue sauce for dipping

Makes 4 servings

Spicy Garlic Chicken Pizza

12 OUNCES BONELESS, SKINLESS
    CHICKEN BREASTS
½ CUP SLICED GREEN ONION, DIVIDED
2 CLOVES GARLIC, MINCED
2 TABLESPOONS WHITE VINEGAR
2 TABLESPOONS SOY SAUCE
3 TABLESPOONS VEGETABLE OIL,
    DIVIDED
¼ TEASPOON CAYENNE PEPPER
¼ TEASPOON BLACK PEPPER

1 TABLESPOON CORNSTARCH
1 TABLESPOON WATER
1 16-OUNCE (12-INCH) ITALIAN BREAD
    SHELL (BOBOLI BRAND) OR TUBE
    OF PIZZA CRUST
½ CUP GRATED MONTEREY JACK
    CHEESE
½ CUP GRATED MOZZARELLA CHEESE
¼ CUP SLIVERED ALMONDS

Cut chicken into 1-inch pieces (kitchen shears work best). In a large bowl combine ¼ cup of the green onion, minced garlic, vinegar, soy sauce, 2 tablespoons of the oil, and the cayenne and black pepper. Add the chicken pieces; stir to coat. Refrigerate the chicken in the marinade for 30 minutes. Drain, reserving marinade.

Heat remaining tablespoon of oil in a large skillet on medium high; add chicken pieces. Cook and stir about 5 to 7 minutes or until no longer pink. Stir cornstarch into the reserved marinade adding the 1 tablespoon of water. Add to skillet. Cook and stir until thickened and bubbly. Cool and freeze. While chicken is cooking, combine the grated cheeses in a 1-quart bag, the remaining ¼ cup of green onions in a 1-quart bag and the almonds in another 1-quart bag. Tape all three bags together to the package of the Italian bread shell.

To prepare for serving, thaw chicken mixture. Preheat oven to 400°F. Spoon mixture evenly atop bread shell. Sprinkle with cheese. Bake, uncovered, for 12 minutes. Top with slivered almonds. Return to oven for 2 minutes more.

Summary of processes: Cut 12 ounces boneless, skinless chicken into 1-inch pieces; slice ½ cup green onion; mince 2 cloves garlic; grate ½ cup Monterey Jack cheese and ½ cup mozzarella cheese
Freeze in: 1-gallon bag; 2 1-quart bags
Serve with: Spinach salad with creamy mustard dressing

Makes 4 servings

Herbed Chicken

2½ TO 3 POUNDS CHICKEN PIECES
1 10¾-OUNCE CAN CREAM OF
    MUSHROOM SOUP
1 TEASPOON GRATED LEMON ZEST
1½ TABLESPOONS LEMON JUICE

½ TEASPOON SALT
1 TEASPOON DRIED BASIL LEAVES
1 TEASPOON DRIED OREGANO LEAVES
RICE (TO SERVE 6)*

Place chicken in a 1-gallon freezer bag. In a small bowl, combine the remaining ingredients, except rice. Pour over the chicken and freeze.

To prepare for serving, thaw chicken mixture. Preheat oven to 350°F. Place mixture in a 13x9x2-inch baking dish, treated with nonstick spray. Bake, covered, for 1¼ hours. Serve over hot, cooked rice.

Summary of processes: Grate 1 tablespoon lemon zest
Freeze in: 1-gallon bag
Serve with: French cut green beans

Makes 6 servings

Country Captain

1 14½-OUNCE CAN STEWED TOMATOES (UNDRAINED)

¼ CUP FRESH PARSLEY, CHOPPED

¼ CUP CURRANTS OR RAISINS

1 TABLESPOON CURRY POWDER

½ CHICKEN BOUILLON CUBE

½ TEASPOON GROUND MACE OR NUTMEG

¼ TEASPOON SUGAR

1 TEASPOON SALT

2½ TO 3 POUNDS COOKED CHICKEN PIECES

1 TABLESPOON CORNSTARCH

1 TABLESPOON COLD WATER

HOT COOKED RICE OR COUSCOUS (TO SERVE 6)*

SLIVERED ALMONDS (OPT.)

In a medium bowl, stir together tomatoes, parsley, currants or raisins, curry powder, bouillon cube, mace or nutmeg, sugar, and salt. Pour over chicken in freezer bag. Label and freeze.

To prepare for serving, place thawed chicken and sauce in large skillet. Bring mixture to a boil; reduce heat. Cover and simmer for 20 minutes or until chicken is no longer pink. Remove chicken from skillet; keep warm. Skim fat from mixture in skillet. In a small bowl stir together cornstarch and cold water; add to skillet. Cook and stir till thickened and bubbly. Cook and stir 2 minutes more. Serve over hot rice or couscous. Sprinkle with almonds, if desired.

Summary of processes: Chop ¼ cup fresh parsley
Freeze in: 1-gallon bag; 1-quart bag
Serve with: Tropical fruit, crescent rolls

Makes 6 servings

Mexican Chicken Lasagna

¾ CUP CHOPPED ONION

3 14-OUNCE CANS STEWED TOMATOES WITH JUICE

½ CUP SALSA, MEDIUM OR MILD

1 1¼-OUNCE PACKAGE TACO SEASONING

1 16-OUNCE CAN BLACK BEANS, RINSED AND DRAINED

1 LARGE EGG

16 OUNCES RICOTTA CHEESE

2 TEASPOONS MINCED GARLIC (2 CLOVES)

10 UNCOOKED LASAGNA NOODLES

4 BONELESS, SKINLESS COOKED CHICKEN BREASTS (ABOUT 1 POUND) CUT INTO 1-INCH CUBES

1 4-OUNCE CAN CHOPPED GREEN CHILIES

1½ CUPS (ABOUT 6 OUNCES) GRATED MONTEREY JACK CHEESE

To make sauce, combine chopped onion with tomatoes, salsa, and taco seasoning. Stir in beans.

To make ricotta layer, whisk egg in small bowl with a fork. Whisk in ricotta cheese and garlic.

Spread 1 cup tomato sauce mixture over the bottom of a greased 13x9x2-inch casserole dish (should barely cover bottom). Top with 5 (uncooked) noodles, overlapping slightly. Spread on one-half of the ricotta cheese mixture. Sprinkle with half the chicken and half the chilies. Spoon 2 cups tomato sauce mixture on top, then add the rest of the ricotta-cheese mixture; spread lightly. Sprinkle with half the grated cheese. Top with remaining noodles, chicken, chilies, tomato sauce mixture, and grated cheese. Cover with foil, label and freeze.

To prepare for serving, thaw and preheat oven to 350°F. Bake, uncovered, for 40 minutes or until noodles are tender when pierced with sharp knife. Cool 10 minutes before serving.

Summary of processes: Chop ¾ cup onion; mince 2 cloves garlic; cut 4 boneless, skinless cooked chicken breasts into 1-inch cubes; grate 1½ cups Monterey Jack cheese
Freeze in: 13x9x2-inch baking dish
Serve with: Slices of avocado and pink grapefruit on lettuce with poppyseed dressing

Makes 8 servings

Sopa de Maíz

2 CUPS CHICKEN BROTH	1 CUP MILK (WHOLE, 2%, OR SKIM)
2 BONELESS, SKINLESS COOKED	SALT AND PEPPER TO TASTE
CHICKEN BREASTS, CHOPPED	FRITOS*
1 16-OUNCE BAG FROZEN CORN	1 TOMATO, CHOPPED*
½ TEASPOON CUMIN	1 AVOCADO, CHOPPED*
1 TEASPOON MINCED GARLIC (1 CLOVE)	SALSA*
2 CHICKEN BOUILLON CUBES	SOUR CREAM (OR PLAIN LOW-FAT
1 4-OUNCE CAN DICED GREEN CHILIES	YOGURT)*

Combine first 7 ingredients in a 6-cup container and freeze.

When preparing to serve, thaw the soup and bring just to boiling. Add milk and simmer until soup is heated through. Season with salt and pepper.

In individual bowls, layer crushed Fritos, chopped tomatoes, and diced avocados. Then pour soup over all. Add dollop each of salsa and sour cream.

Summary of processes: Chop 2 boneless, skinless cooked chicken breasts
Freeze in: 6-cup container
Serve with: Taco salad

Makes 5 to 6 servings

Biscuit Beef Bake

1 POUND LEAN GROUND BEEF	1 8-OUNCE CAN TOMATO SAUCE
½ CUP ONION, CHOPPED	½ CUP FROZEN CORN
1 TEASPOON MINCED GARLIC (1 CLOVE)	2 TEASPOONS CHILI POWDER
1 14½-OUNCE CAN MEXICAN-STYLE	1 TEASPOON CUMIN
STEWED TOMATOES, UNDRAINED	1 TEASPOON SALT
1 15-OUNCE CAN BLACK BEANS, RINSED	1 12-OUNCE PACKAGE HUNGRY JACK
AND DRAINED	BUTTERMILK BISCUITS*

Brown ground beef with the onion and garlic in a 10-inch skillet over medium heat until meat is no longer pink, about 10 minutes (or use 2½ cups already-browned ground beef). Stir in the remaining ingredients, except biscuits. Bring to a boil and simmer for 10 minutes. Cool. Package in 5-cup container, label and freeze. Store the tube of Hungry Jack biscuits in the refrigerator.

When preparing to serve, thaw and preheat oven to 400°F. Transfer the mixture to a 8x8-inch ovenproof dish that has been treated with nonstick spray. Arrange the biscuits on top and bake for 15 to 20 minutes.

Summary of processes: Chop ½ cup onion; mince 1 clove garlic
Freeze in: 5-cup container
Serve with: baked apples

Makes 6 servings

French Stuffed Potatoes

1 POUND LEAN GROUND BEEF
¼ CUP CHOPPED GREEN ONION
1 4-OUNCE CAN MUSHROOM PIECES
    AND STEMS
½ TEASPOON SALT

½ TEASPOON ONION SALT
½ CUP EACH GRATED SWISS AND
    CHEDDAR CHEESE
4 LARGE BAKING POTATOES*

Brown together in a skillet the ground beef, green onion, and mushrooms (add a tablespoon of water if mixture is too dry), about 10 minutes. Add the salt and onion salt.

Freeze the meat mixture in a freezer bag. Store the grated cheese in a small bag and slip the smaller bag into the larger one; store in freezer. Store the potatoes in the pantry (don't freeze or refrigerate raw potatoes).

When preparing to serve, thaw the meat mixture and cheeses. Preheat oven to 400°F. Wash and prick the potatoes and bake for 1 hour or until done. When potatoes are nearly done, heat the meat mixture in a small saucepan or skillet.

Slice open the potatoes, break up potatoes with a fork, and spoon the meat mixture and cheese atop each potato. Return to the oven until cheese is melted.

Summary of processes: Chop ¼ cup green onions; grate ½ cup cheddar cheese; grate ½ cup Swiss cheese
Freeze in: 1-gallon bag; 1-quart bag
Serve with: Sliced tomatoes, Caesar salad

Makes 4 servings

Poppy Turkey

2 POUNDS GROUND TURKEY
½ CUP CHOPPED GREEN PEPPER
½ TEASPOON SALT
½ CUP CHOPPED ONION
1 15-OUNCE CAN TOMATO SAUCE
1 CUP LOW-FAT COTTAGE CHEESE
1 TABLESPOON POPPY SEEDS

1 CUP PLAIN LOW-FAT YOGURT
1 8-OUNCE PACKAGE LIGHT CREAM
    CHEESE
¼ TEASPOON PEPPER
8 OUNCES LINGUINE*
¼ CUP GRATED PARMESAN CHEESE*

Sauté the turkey with green pepper, salt, and onion in a large skillet on medium heat until the turkey is no longer pink, about 15 minutes. Add tomato sauce and set aside. Combine the remaining ingredients in a medium bowl, except linguine and Parmesan cheese. Freeze each of the two mixtures in 1-gallon bags taped together.

When preparing to serve, thaw the bags. Preheat oven to 350°F. Cook 8 ounces linguine according to package directions and drain. While pasta is hot, mix it into the cheese mixture in a medium bowl. Spread the linguine and cheese on the bottom of a greased casserole dish. Top with the meat mixture and sprinkle with Parmesan cheese. Bake for 30 minutes or until hot and bubbly.

Summary of processes: Chop ½ cup green pepper; chop ½ cup onion
Freeze in: 2 1-gallon bags
Serve with: Green beans, Cheesy-Herb Bread (page 135)

Makes 10 servings

Playoff Burgers

2 POUNDS LEAN GROUND BEEF

1 ONION, CHOPPED

1 TABLESPOON A-1 SAUCE

¼ POUND GRATED MONTEREY JACK
    CHEESE

SALT AND PEPPER TO TASTE

6 WHOLE WHEAT BUNS*

Salt and pepper ground beef to taste and mix with chopped onion and A-1 sauce. Make 12 thin patties. Sprinkle cheese over 6 of these, then top with remaining 6 patties and press edges together. Wrap each patty in waxed paper and seal them in a 1-gallon freezer bag. Label the bag and freeze. Freeze the package of whole wheat buns.

To prepare for serving, thaw patties and place on the rack of a broiler pan. Broil 3 to 4 inches from the heat for a total of 12 to 14 minutes or until done, turning once. Serve on thawed whole wheat buns, split and toasted.

Summary of processes: Grate ¼ pound Monterey Jack cheese; chop 1 onion
Freeze in: 1-gallon bag
Serve with: Carrot sticks, baked beans, watermelon
Note: Great on the grill or for camping trips.

Makes 6 servings

London Broil

1 LONDON BROIL OR FLANK STEAK (ABOUT 2 POUNDS)	1 TABLESPOON VEGETABLE OIL
	1 CLOVE GARLIC, MINCED
1 TEASPOON GROUND GINGER	1 TEASPOON BLACK PEPPER
1 TABLESPOON GRATED LEMON ZEST	1 TEASPOON BROWN SUGAR

In a shallow bowl, large enough to hold the steak, stir all other ingredients together, making a marinade. Turn the steak in the marinade, rubbing the ingredients into the meat. Put steak and marinade in a freezer bag, label and freeze.

To prepare for serving, thaw steak and discard marinade. Grill over hot coals 4 to 5 minutes per side. Do not overcook or flank steak becomes tough (serving rare is best). Carve slices on the bias.

Freeze in: 1-cup freezer container
Serve with: Baked potato, Fresh-Baked Asparagus (page 151)

Makes 5 servings

Farmer's Casserole

6 CUPS FROZEN SHREDDED HASH BROWN POTATOES	4 BEATEN EGGS
	1 12-OUNCE CAN EVAPORATED MILK OR
1 CUP GRATED MONTEREY JACK CHEESE WITH JALAPEÑO PEPPERS	EVAPORATED SKIM MILK (1½ CUPS)
1 CUP DICED FULLY COOKED HAM	⅛ TEASPOON PEPPER
¼ CUP SLICED GREEN ONION	¼ TEASPOON SALT

Grease a 13x9x2-inch baking dish. Arrange potatoes evenly in the bottom of the dish. Sprinkle with cheese, ham, and green onion.

In a medium mixing bowl combine eggs, evaporated milk, pepper, and salt. Pour egg mixture over potato mixture in dish. Freeze.

To prepare to serve, thaw and preheat oven to 350°F. Bake, uncovered, for 40 to 45 minutes or until center appears set. Let stand 5 minutes before serving.

Summary of processes: Grate 1 cup Monterey Jack cheese with jalapeño peppers; dice 1 cup ham; slice ¼ cup green onions

Freeze in: 13x9x2-inch baking dish
Serve with: Wedges of cantaloupe and Apple-Date Freezer Coffee Cake (page 140)

Makes 12 servings

Crab Shells

6 TABLESPOONS BUTTER OR
    MARGARINE, DIVIDED
3 GREEN ONIONS, CHOPPED (½ CUP)
½ TEASPOON WORCESTERSHIRE SAUCE
1 TEASPOON DIJON MUSTARD
½ POUND CRABMEAT (OR IMITATION),
    CHOPPED SMALL (THAWED IF
    PURCHASED FROZEN)

SALT AND PEPPER TO TASTE
12 JUMBO PASTA SHELLS
4 TABLESPOONS ALL-PURPOSE FLOUR
2½ CUPS MILK (WHOLE, 2%, OR SKIM)
½ CUP GRATED PARMESAN CHEESE,
    DIVIDED

In a small saucepan or skillet melt 2 tablespoons of the butter or margarine. Add chopped green onion, Worcestershire sauce, mustard, crabmeat, and salt and pepper to taste. Stir over medium heat until heated through. Fill pasta shells with mixture and arrange shells in round baking dish that has been treated with nonstick spray.

In same skillet melt the remaining 4 tablespoons butter. Stir in flour. Remove from heat and gradually whisk in milk. Return to a boil and cook for 3 minutes, stirring. Stir in salt and pepper and ¼ cup of the Parmesan cheese, stirring until the cheese melts. Pour sauce over shells and top with remaining cheese. Cover with foil, label and freeze.

To prepare for serving, thaw and preheat oven to 400°F. Bake, covered, for 30 minutes.

Summary of processes: Chop 3 green onions; chop crabmeat
Freeze in: 10-inch round baking dish
Serve with: Cucumber salad

Makes 4 to 5 servings

❏

CHAPTER 5

The Cross Country:
A One-Month Entrée Plan

❏

GROCERY SHOPPING AND STAPLES LISTS

An asterisk (*) after an item indicates that it can be stored until you cook the dish with which it will be served. For example, the spaghetti will not be cooked until the day you serve Spaghetti. Mark those items with an X as a reminder that you'll need them for an entrée.

When entrées require perishable foods to be refrigerated until served, you may want to use those dishes right away or buy the food the week you plan to prepare the dish. For example, fresh mushrooms would spoil by the end of a month.

For this one-month entrée plan, you will need these food items as well as the ones in the staples list that follows.

Grocery Shopping List

Canned Goods

    1 8¾-ounce can apricots

    1 14½-ounce can beef broth

    1 8-ounce bottle chili sauce

    2 10¾-ounce cans condensed cream of mushroom soup (1 can)*

    1 12-ounce can evaporated skim milk

THE CROSS COUNTRY:
A ONE-MONTH ENTRÉE PLAN

SUN.	MON.	TUES.	WED.	THURS.	FRI.	SAT.
1 Eat Out Cooking Day!	2 Manicotti	3 Chinese Chicken Morsels	4 Veal Scaloppine in Spaghetti Sauce	5 Teriyaki Burgers	6 Ham and Swiss Pastry Bake	7 Baked Eggs
8 Cheesy Corn Casserole	9 Poulet de France	10 Mimi's Chicken Soup	11 Joes to Go	12 Winter Barley	13 Bacon-Wrapped Burgers	14 Meal-in-One Potatoes
15 Hot Brisket Sandwiches	16 Spaghetti	17 Chicken Packets	18 Aztec Quiche	19 Wild Rice Chicken	20 Taco Pie	21 Linguine à la Anne
22 Stove-Top Barbecued Chicken	23 French Bread Pizza	24 Ham Dinner Slices	25 Ravioli Soup	26 Heavenly Chicken	27 Mrs. Ringle's Brisket	28 Baked Herb Fish Fillets
29 Teriyaki Chicken	30 Fruity Curried Chicken					

2 4-ounce cans diced, green chilies
1 15-ounce can red kidney beans
1 17-ounce can whole kernel corn
1 2-ounce and 1 4-ounce can mushroom stems and pieces
1 15-ounce can tomatoes
4 28-ounce cans Italian-style or plain crushed tomatoes in puree
1 12-ounce and 1 6-ounce can tomato paste
3 8-ounce cans tomato sauce
1 8-ounce can sliced water chestnuts

Grains, Pasta, and Rice

7 bread slices
1 loaf unsliced French bread (not sourdough)*
6 hamburger buns*
8 to 10 sandwich rolls*
1 8-ounce container Italian-flavored bread crumbs*
1 12-ounce package linguine
1 8-ounce package manicotti
1 16-ounce package spaghetti*
1 8-ounce package spinach or wide egg noodles*
1 8-ounce package tortellini*
1 12-ounce package seasoned bread stuffing—7-pound bird size (6 cups)
1 6¼-ounce package long grain and wild rice (Uncle Ben's Fast Cooking Long Grain and Wild Rice, if available)
1 32-ounce package regular rice
Quick-cooking barley (need ¾ cup)

Dry Ingredients and Seasonings

⅓ cup raisins
1 package onion soup mix
1 envelope taco seasoning mix
1½ cups (about) seasoned croutons (1 cup croutons, ½ cup crushed)

Frozen Foods

4 frozen fish fillets (about 1¼ pounds) (orange roughy or sole)
2 9-inch deep-dish frozen pie shells (1*)
1 12-ounce package plain ravioli without sauce* (located in the frozen or refrigerated section)
1 10-ounce package frozen, chopped spinach

Dairy Products

1 cup (about) margarine
1 8-ounce carton small-curd, low-fat cottage cheese with chives

1 16-ounce carton small-curd, low-fat cottage cheese

2 packages refrigerated crescent rolls*

19 eggs

1 cup half-and-half

2 quarts milk (whole, 2%, or skim)

18 ounces (4½ cups) grated, mild cheddar cheese

1 3-ounce package cream cheese

5 ounces (1¼ cups) grated Monterey Jack cheese

16 ounces (4 cups) mozzarella cheese (4 slices, remaining grated)

12 ounces (about 3 cups) grated Parmesan cheese

1 15-ounce container part-skim ricotta cheese

2 ounces (½ cup) grated Romano cheese

4 ounces (1 cup) grated Swiss cheese

1 8-ounce carton sour cream or plain low-fat yogurt

Note: See Chapter 10 for ounce/cup equivalent measures.

Meat and Poultry

1 4-to-6-pound beef brisket

8 pounds lean ground beef (allow 1 pound for hamburgers; buy more if needed for your family)

½ pound ground turkey

9 pounds whole chickens or 7 pounds breasts

5¾ pounds boneless, skinless chicken breasts

2 pounds chicken pieces (breasts, drumsticks, or thighs)

4 strips bacon

5 to 6 pounds boneless, cooked ham, with 3 pounds cubed, and the center portion cut in dinner slices

1 pound bulk Italian sausage

1 pound very thin, boneless veal cutlets* (or substitute 1 pound boneless, skinless chicken breasts)

3-ounce package (use ½) sliced pepperoni

Produce

3 medium carrots

1 bunch celery

1 whole head garlic (10 cloves)

1 small lemon*

1 small head of lettuce

1 small bunch green onions

2 medium green bell peppers

1 medium red bell pepper

6 pounds (about 9) yellow onions
1 bunch fresh parsley

Staples List

Make sure you have the following staples on hand; add those you don't have to your shopping list.

basil leaves, dried
bay leaves
biscuit baking mix (1 cup)
brown sugar (about ¾ cup)
catsup (⅓ cup)
cayenne pepper
celery seeds
chicken bouillon cube
chili powder
cinnamon, ground
cloves (whole)
cumin, ground
curry powder
flour, all-purpose
garlic powder
garlic salt
ginger, ground
lemon juice (about ⅔ cup)
8 medium baking potatoes*
8 to 10 new potatoes*
3 tomatoes*
lemon pepper
marjoram
light mayonnaise (about 2 cups)
minced onion
Dijon mustard (¼ cup)
dried mustard (1 teaspoon)
prepared mustard
nonstick spray
onion salt
dried oregano leaves
pepper
salt
soda crackers (1 cup crumbs)
soy sauce (¾ cup)
sugar

dried thyme leaves
vegetable oil
red wine vinegar
white vinegar
waxed paper
Worcestershire sauce

FREEZER CONTAINERS

The following list of freezer containers or flat baking dishes will be needed for the entrées. These are not the only containers you can use, but this list gives you an idea of the size and number of containers you'll need.

Heavy Aluminum Foil
French Bread Pizza

15 1-Quart Freezer Bags
French Bread Pizza (3); Linguine à la Anne (2); Chicken Packets (2); Veal Scaloppine in Spaghetti Sauce (2); Heavenly Chicken; Poulet de France; Taco Pie; Cheesy Corn Casserole; Meal-in-One Potatoes; Baked Herb Fish Fillets

13 1-Gallon Freezer Bags
Mrs. Ringle's Brisket; Hot Brisket Sandwiches; Veal Scaloppine; Ham and Swiss Pastry Bake; Wild Rice Chicken; Chinese Chicken Morsels; Bacon-Wrapped Burgers; Ham Dinner Slices; Teriyaki Burgers; Teriyaki Chicken; Baked Herb Fish Fillets; Stove-Top Barbecued Chicken; Winter Barley

2 3-Cup Containers
Veal Scaloppine in Spaghetti Sauce; French Bread Pizza

2 4-Cup Containers
Fruity Curried Chicken, Spaghetti Sauce

2 8-Cup Containers
Joes to Go; Mimi's Chicken Soup

1 10-Cup Container
  Ravioli Soup

1 8x8x2-Inch Baking Dish
  Cheesy Corn Casserole

4 13x9x2-Inch Baking Dishes
  Linguine à la Anne; Heavenly Chicken; Poulet de France; Baked Eggs

1 3-Quart Casserole of Any Shape
  Manicotti

1 9-Inch Quiche or Pie Pan
  Aztec Quiche

1 10-Inch Quiche or Pie Pan
  Taco Pie

THE DAY BEFORE COOKING DAY

1. Cut 1½ pounds of boneless chicken breasts into 1-inch cubes with kitchen scissors and refrigerate. Refrigerate remaining boneless chicken breasts and 2 pounds of chicken pieces.
2. Refrigerate lemon and store baking and new potatoes (unrefrigerated) until you're ready to serve them.
3. Place 9 pounds whole chickens (or 7 pounds breasts) in about 6 quarts water in a large pot (you may need two). Bring to a boil; reduce heat. Cover and simmer until thickest pieces are done, about 45 minutes to 1 hour. Save and refrigerate 3¼ quarts chicken broth.
    Cool chicken until ready to handle. Remove meat from bones and skin. Cut chicken into bite-size pieces using kitchen scissors, which are easier to use than a knife. Refrigerate chicken pieces in two plastic bags.
4. Put ham dinner slices, hamburger buns, and sandwich rolls in freezer bags; mark bags with names of recipes; store them in freezer until you're ready to serve them.
5. For Veal Scaloppine in Spaghetti Sauce, put veal cutlets in 1-gallon bag, Italian-flavored bread crumbs and mozzarella cheese in separate 1-quart bags; freeze them together.
6. For French Bread Pizza, put pepperoni in 1-quart freezer bag, ¼ cup grated Parme-

san cheese and 1 cup grated mozzarella cheese in separate 1-quart freezer bags; wrap French bread in heavy foil and put them together in freezer.

7. Set out appliances, bowls, canned goods, dry ingredients, freezer containers, and recipes.

8. Start Mrs. Ringle's Brisket in a Crock-Pot (just before bed).

COOKING DAY ASSEMBLY ORDER

Make sure you've cleared the table and counters of unnecessary kitchenware to allow plenty of working room. It also helps to have fresh, damp washcloths and towels for wiping your hands and the cooking area. The day will go a lot more smoothly if you keep cleaning and organizing as you work.

Before you prepare a recipe, gather all the spices and ingredients in the assembly area to save time and steps. When you finish the recipe, remove unneeded items and wipe off the work space.

BEFORE ASSEMBLING DISHES

1. Cool, slice, and divide brisket and gravy in half for Mrs. Ringle's Brisket and Hot Brisket Sandwiches. Put brisket in two 1-gallon bags and freeze them. Wash out Crock-Pot.

2. Skim and discard fat from chicken broth.

3. Perform all chopping, crushing, grating, and slicing tasks.

   Ham: Cut 8 cups into cubes.

   Onions: Leave one onion whole for Mimi's Chicken Soup; finely chop remaining onions. Open windows, and keep tissues handy. Store onions in cold water in a container with a tight lid.

   Green onions: Chop ½ cup.

   Green bell peppers: Finely chop 1; slice 1.

   Red bell pepper: Slice 1.

   Carrots: Shred 3.

   Celery: Slice ½ cup with leaves; finely chop 1¾ cups.

   Garlic: Mince 8½ teaspoons (8½ cloves).

   Parsley: Chop ⅔ cup.

   Mozzarella cheese: Cut 4 slices; grate the rest.

   Monterey Jack cheese: Grate all.

   Mild cheddar cheese: Grate all.

   Cracker crumbs: Crush 1 cup.

4. Start Spaghetti Sauce.
5. Spray pans or baking dishes you will need with nonstick spray (check list of freezer containers on pages 74–75).
6. As you assemble the ham, chicken, beef, and miscellaneous entrées, allow them to cool if necessary, put them in storage containers, and freeze them.

Assemble Ham Dishes

1. Boil linguine according to the package directions, setting timer.
2. Finish preparing Linguine à la Anne.
3. Assemble Ham and Swiss Pastry Bake.
4. Freeze ham dishes.

Assemble Poultry Dishes

1. Prepare Stove-Top Barbecued Chicken in a skillet, and simmer.
2. In separate saucepans, cook rice for Wild Rice Chicken and the ¾ cup regular rice for Fruity Curried Chicken according to package directions.
3. Make filling for Chicken Packets in a medium bowl (mixing with hands works best), and put in a freezer bag.
4. Finish assembling Wild Rice Chicken and Fruity Curried Chicken.
5. Prepare Heavenly Chicken.
6. Prepare Chinese Chicken Morsels.
7. Assemble Poulet de France.
8. Assemble filling for Meal-in-One Potatoes.
9. Assemble Teriyaki Chicken.
10. Prepare Mimi's Chicken Soup with remaining chicken broth and start simmering.
11. Freeze poultry dishes.

Assemble Miscellaneous Dishes

1. Prepare Baked Herb Fish Fillets coating mix.
2. Complete Aztec Quiche.
3. Prepare Baked Eggs. (If you use bacon for Baked Eggs, at the same time you fry it, fry 5 more slices till limp, and set aside for Bacon-Wrapped Burgers.)
4. Cool Spaghetti Sauce.
5. Freeze miscellaneous dishes.

Assemble Beef Dishes

1. Cook manicotti according to package directions.
2. Assemble Teriyaki Burgers.

3. Complete Bacon-Wrapped Burgers.
4. Drain manicotti; rinse with cold water. Separate manicotti noodles; put each on waxed paper.
5. In a large skillet, cook and stir 6 pounds lean ground beef until brown, about 30 minutes.
6. In a small skillet, sauté ⅓ and ¾ cups chopped onions until tender; use for Taco Pie and Joes to Go.
7. Assemble Ravioli Soup, starting it simmering.
8. Finish Manicotti.
9. Put Spaghetti Sauce in freezer containers according to directions. Put containers of sauce for Veal Scaloppine in Spaghetti Sauce and French Bread Pizza in freezer with already packaged items for those dishes.
10. Assemble Taco Pie.
11. Prepare Joes to Go and Winter Barley.
12. Complete Cheesy Corn Casserole.
13. Allow Mimi's Chicken Soup and Ravioli Soup to cool and store in freezer containers.
14. Freeze beef dishes.

You made it! Hooray!!

RECIPES FOR THE ONE-MONTH ENTRÉE PLAN

Each recipe offers complete instructions on how to prepare the dish. Food items with an asterisk (*) won't be prepared until you serve the entrée. For recipes calling for oven baking, preheat oven for about 10 minutes.

"Summary of processes" gives a quick overview of foods that need to be chopped, diced, grated, or sliced. "Freeze in" tells what bags and containers will be needed to freeze each entrée. "Serve with" offers suggestions of foods to accompany the meal. Some of the recipes for those foods are included in Chapter 8; page numbers are indicated for easy reference. "Note" includes special instructions on how the entrée can be used in other ways.

Mrs. Ringle's Brisket

1 4-TO-6 POUND BRISKET	4 TO 5 NEW POTATOES*
2 TABLESPOONS PREPARED MUSTARD	FLOUR (OPT.)
1 PACKAGE ONION SOUP MIX	

Place brisket fat side up in a Crock-Pot. Do not add any water or liquid. Cover brisket with mustard and dry onion soup mix. Cook on low overnight.

Skim mustard and onion seasoning from brisket and mix it with juice in the Crock-Pot. Remove brisket from Crock-Pot; allow to cool. Peel off fat and discard it; slice or shred meat. Save juices and seasonings (thicken with flour to make gravy if desired). Divide meat and gravy in half, and store in separate 1-gallon bags in freezer. Reserve 1 bag for Mrs. Ringle's Brisket and one for Hot Brisket Sandwiches.

To prepare for serving, thaw brisket and gravy and heat. At the same time, prepare new potatoes. Heat 1 cup salted water to a boil; add potatoes. Cover and heat until boiling; reduce heat. Simmer tightly covered until tender, 20 to 25 minutes; drain. Serve potatoes with brisket and gravy.

Freeze in: 2 1-gallon bags
Serve with: Cheese grits, Cranberry Cream Salad (page 147)

Makes 4 to 5 servings

Hot Brisket Sandwiches

HALF OF GRAVY AND SLICED BRISKET	MARGARINE OR MAYONNAISE FOR
4 TO 6 SANDWICH ROLLS	ROLLS

Thaw brisket slices; heat them in the gravy. Serve on warm sandwich rolls. Serve gravy on the side for dipping.

Serve with: Cinnamon Applesauce Salad (page 147) and celery slices

Makes 4 to 6 servings

Spaghetti Sauce

1 POUND BULK ITALIAN SAUSAGE

1½ CUPS FINELY CHOPPED ONION

1 12-OUNCE CAN TOMATO PASTE

3 28-OUNCE CANS ITALIAN-STYLE OR
    PLAIN CRUSHED TOMATOES IN
    PUREE

2 CUPS WATER

4 TEASPOONS MINCED GARLIC
    (4 CLOVES)

4 BAY LEAVES

2 TABLESPOONS SUGAR

4 TEASPOONS DRIED BASIL LEAVES

2 TEASPOONS DRIED OREGANO LEAVES

4 TABLESPOONS CHOPPED FRESH
    PARSLEY

2 TEASPOONS SALT

1 16-OUNCE PACKAGE SPAGHETTI*

In a large pot, cook and stir the bulk Italian sausage with onions until the meat is brown, about 15 minutes, drain fat. Add remaining ingredients, except the spaghetti. Bring sauce to a boil; reduce heat. Partly cover and simmer for 2 hours, stirring occasionally. (If desired, simmer in a Crock-Pot instead of pot.) Makes 12 cups sauce.

Allow sauce to cool. Freeze in separate containers for Spaghetti (4 cups); Veal Scaloppine in Spaghetti Sauce (2½ cups); and French Bread Pizza (3 cups). Reserve 2½ cups sauce for Manicotti.

To prepare Spaghetti, thaw 4 cups sauce, and heat in a medium saucepan. At the same time, cook spaghetti according to package directions, drain, and pour sauce over them.

Summary of processes: Chop 1½ cups onions, 4 tablespoons parsley; mince 4 cloves garlic

Freeze in: 4-cup container, Spaghetti; 2 3-cup containers French Bread Pizza and Veal Scaloppine in Spaghetti Sauce; reserve 2½ cups for Manicotti

Serve with: Jiffy Salad (page 147), garlic bread

Makes 6 servings

Veal Scaloppine in Spaghetti Sauce

1 POUND THIN VEAL CUTLETS (OR
    SUBSTITUTE 1 POUND BONELESS,
    SKINLESS CHICKEN BREASTS)*
2½ CUPS SPAGHETTI SAUCE*
1 EGG*
¾ CUP ITALIAN-FLAVORED BREAD
    CRUMBS*

3 TABLESPOONS VEGETABLE OR OLIVE
    OIL*
1 TEASPOON MINCED GARLIC
    (1 CLOVE)*
4 SLICES MOZZARELLA CHEESE*
GRATED PARMESAN CHEESE*

This recipe is assembled on the day it's served. Put veal cutlets in 1-gallon bag; Spaghetti Sauce in a 3-cup container; Italian-flavored bread crumbs and mozzarella cheese in separate 1-quart bags; freeze them together.

Thaw veal cutlets, bread crumbs, cheese slices, and container of Spaghetti Sauce. Beat egg with fork until white and yolk are blended. Sprinkle Italian-flavored bread crumbs on a sheet of waxed paper. Dip veal into egg and then crumbs, turning to coat both sides evenly.

In a large skillet, heat oil with garlic over medium or medium-high heat. Add veal; sauté 4 minutes on each side, until golden brown. Top each piece of veal with a cheese slice. Pour Spaghetti Sauce around veal. Bring sauce to boil; reduce heat. Cover and simmer 5 minutes or until cheese is melted. Sprinkle Parmesan cheese on top.

Summary of processes: Mince 1 clove garlic; slice 4 slices mozzarella cheese
Freeze in: 3-cup container, 1-gallon bag, and 2 1-quart bags
Serve with: Tossed green salad, Dawn's French Bread (page 138)

Makes 4 servings

French Bread Pizza

1 LOAF UNSLICED FRENCH BREAD (NOT
    SOURDOUGH)*
3 CUPS SPAGHETTI SAUCE*
¼ CUP GRATED PARMESAN CHEESE*

1 CUP GRATED MOZZARELLA CHEESE*
3 OUNCES PEPPERONI SLICES (HALF A
    PACKAGE)*

This recipe is assembled on the day it's served. Put sauce in a 3-cup container, cheeses in 2 1-quart bags, pepperoni in 1-quart bag; wrap bread in heavy foil. Freeze them together.

To prepare for serving, thaw French bread, sauce, grated cheeses, and pepperoni. Slice loaf of French bread in half lengthwise. Layer sauce, Parmesan cheese, pepperoni, and mozzarella cheese on each half. Set oven to broil and/or 550°F. Place bread on baking sheet and put in the oven. Broil until mozzarella is melted. Cut into serving-size pieces.

Summary of processes: Grate 4 ounces mozzarella cheese
Freeze in: 3-cup container; 3 1-quart bags; foil for bread
Serve with: Waldorf salad

Makes 6 to 8 servings

Linguine à la Anne

1 12-OUNCE PACKAGE LINGUINE

1⅓ CUPS WATER

1 CHICKEN BOUILLON CUBE

Sauce

2 TABLESPOONS MARGARINE

2 TABLESPOONS ALL-PURPOSE FLOUR

½ TEASPOON SALT

1 12-OUNCE CAN EVAPORATED SKIM
    MILK

1 4-OUNCE CAN MUSHROOM STEMS AND
    PIECES (RESERVE LIQUID)

4 CUPS COOKED, CUBED HAM

½ CUP GRATED ROMANO CHEESE

1 SLICED RED BELL PEPPER

1 SLICED GREEN BELL PEPPER

1 TABLESPOON VEGETABLE OIL

1 CUP SEASONED CROUTONS*

Cook linguine in a large pot according to package directions, drain, and return to pot. While linguine cooks, melt margarine in a medium saucepan over low heat. Stir in flour and salt, adding evaporated milk. Bring to a boil, stirring constantly. Boil and stir 1 minute. Add liquid from mushrooms, water, and the bouillon cube. Cook over medium heat, stirring constantly, until bubbly and slightly thickened.

Add 2 cups of the sauce and drained mushrooms to linguine and toss until well mixed. Spoon linguine mixture into a 13x9x2-inch baking dish, pressing it up the sides to leave a slight hollow in center of dish.

Toss ham in remaining sauce; spread it in the center of the linguine. Sprinkle with Romano cheese; cover with foil and freeze dish. Sauté red and green bell peppers in vegetable oil until soft, about 10 minutes; allow to cool. Put peppers in 1-quart freezer bag; attach this bag and croutons in a 1-quart freezer bag to the dish.

To prepare for serving, thaw dish, peppers, and croutons. Bake dish uncovered in a preheated 400°F oven for 20 minutes. Before serving, sprinkle croutons around edge of casserole. Reheat sautéed red and green bell peppers and mound them in the center.

Summary of processes: Cut ham into cubes; slice 1 red bell pepper and 1 green bell pepper

Freeze in: 13x9x2-inch baking dish; 2 1-quart bags

Serve with: Cooked zucchini, Orange Spiced Tea (page 143)

Note: Great for company that includes children.

Makes 8 servings

Ham and Swiss Pastry Bake

2 CUPS COOKED, CUBED HAM

1 CUP GRATED SWISS CHEESE

¼ CUP FINELY CHOPPED CELERY

¼ CUP FINELY CHOPPED GREEN BELL
   PEPPER

2 TABLESPOONS MINCED ONION

1 TEASPOON DRIED MUSTARD

1 TABLESPOON LEMON JUICE

⅓ CUP LIGHT MAYONNAISE OR SALAD
   DRESSING*

1 9-INCH DEEP-DISH, FROZEN PIE
   SHELL*

Combine ham, cheese, celery, bell pepper, onion, mustard, and lemon juice in a 1-gallon plastic bag and store in freezer.

To prepare for serving, thaw ham mixture, add mayonnaise, and put into a 9-inch pie shell. Bake uncovered in a preheated 375°F oven for 25 to 35 minutes until golden brown. Serve hot.

Summary of processes: Cut 2 cups ham into cubes; grate 1 cup Swiss cheese; chop ¼ cup celery and ¼ cup bell pepper

Freeze in: 1-gallon bag

Serve with: Frozen Fruit Medley (page 148)

Makes 6 servings

Stove-Top Barbecued Chicken

1 TEASPOON VEGETABLE OIL
1 CUP FINELY CHOPPED ONION
⅓ CUP CATSUP
⅓ CUP WATER
4 TEASPOONS WHITE VINEGAR
4 TEASPOONS BROWN SUGAR
1½ TEASPOONS WORCESTERSHIRE
    SAUCE

½ TEASPOON CHILI POWDER
¼ TEASPOON CRUSHED CELERY SEEDS
2 POUNDS SKINLESS CHICKEN PIECES
1 8-OUNCE PACKAGE SPINACH OR WIDE
    EGG NOODLES*

Heat oil in a large, nonstick skillet; sauté onion until tender, about 10 minutes. Stir in catsup, water, vinegar, brown sugar, Worcestershire sauce, chili powder, and celery seeds. Bring sauce to a boil. Add the chicken to the skillet, placing the side down that has the skin removed; spoon sauce over the pieces. Bring to a boil; reduce heat. Cover and simmer 30 minutes. Turn chicken pieces and simmer covered for about 20 minutes more or until chicken is cooked through. Cool and freeze chicken and sauce.

To prepare for serving, thaw chicken and sauce; put in a large skillet and cook over medium heat, stirring constantly until bubbly. Cook package of spinach or egg noodles according to package directions; serve chicken over noodles.

Summary of processes: Chop 1 cup onion
Freeze in: 4-cup container
Serve with: Corn on the cob, Low-Calorie Chocolate Cake (page 145)

Makes 4 servings

Chicken Packets

2 CUPS COOKED, CHOPPED CHICKEN
1 3-OUNCE PACKAGE CREAM CHEESE,
    SOFTENED
1 TABLESPOON CHOPPED CHIVES
2 TABLESPOONS MILK (WHOLE, 2%, OR
    SKIM)

SALT TO TASTE
½ CUP CRUSHED, SEASONED CROUTON
    CRUMBS*
2 PACKAGES REFRIGERATED CRESCENT
    ROLLS*
¼ CUP MELTED MARGARINE*

Mix chicken, cream cheese, chives, milk, and salt in a medium bowl (mixing with hands works best) to make filling and store in a 1-quart freezer bag. Put crouton crumbs in another 1-quart bag, attach it to bag of chicken filling, and freeze them. Refrigerate crescent rolls.

To prepare for serving, thaw chicken mixture. Unroll crescent rolls. Each tube will contain 4 rectangles of dough with a diagonal perforation. Press dough along each perforation so that the rectangle halves will not separate. Place about ¼ cup of chicken mixture into the center of each rectangle. Fold dough over the filling, and pinch the edges to seal tightly. Dip each packet in melted margarine and coat with crouton crumbs. Place packets on a baking sheet. Bake in a preheated 350°F oven for 20 minutes or until golden brown. Packets are good either hot or cold. (Serve early in the month before date expires on crescent rolls.) Makes 8 packets.

Summary of processes: Chop 2 cups cooked chicken and 1 tablespoon chives
Freeze in: 2 1-quart bags
Serve with: Smoky Corn Chowder (page 149), baked apples stuffed with plump raisins
Note: These packets are a favorite with children.

Makes 4 to 6 servings

Wild Rice Chicken

1 6¼-OUNCE PACKAGE QUICK-COOKING, LONG GRAIN AND WILD RICE
1 CUP COOKED, CHOPPED CHICKEN
1 8-OUNCE CAN SLICED WATER CHESTNUTS, DRAINED
1 CUP FINELY CHOPPED CELERY
1¼ CUPS FINELY CHOPPED ONION
1 CUP LIGHT MAYONNAISE*
1 10¾-OUNCE CAN CONDENSED CREAM OF MUSHROOM SOUP*

Cook rice according to package directions. Combine rice with chopped chicken, water chestnuts, celery, and onion; put mixture in a 1-gallon freezer bag.

To prepare for serving, thaw rice and chicken mixture, remove from bag, and place in a 2½ quart baking dish. Stir mayonnaise and condensed cream of mushroom soup together and spread over top of chicken. Bake covered in a preheated 325°F oven for 1 hour.

Summary of processes: Chop 1 cup cooked chicken, 1 cup celery, and 1¼ cups onion
Freeze in: 1-gallon bag
Serve with: Cooked green beans, peach halves with cottage cheese topped with a maraschino cherry.

Makes 6 servings

Fruity Curried Chicken

¾ CUP REGULAR, UNCOOKED RICE

1 CUP FINELY CHOPPED ONION

2½ CUPS CHICKEN BROTH

1 8¾-OUNCE CAN APRICOTS, DRAINED

2¼ CUPS COOKED, DICED CHICKEN

¾ TEASPOON SALT

¼ TEASPOON CURRY POWDER

¼ TEASPOON PEPPER

2 TEASPOONS LEMON JUICE

⅓ CUP RAISINS

In a medium saucepan, bring rice, onion, and chicken broth to a boil, stirring once or twice. Reduce heat to low; cover and simmer 15 minutes. Do not lift lid or stir rice. Drain and cut apricots into pieces. Add the remaining ingredients. Allow to cool and store in freezer.

To prepare for serving, thaw entrée, put in baking dish, and cover with foil. Bake in a preheated 350°F oven for 1 hour. (Add a small amount of water if it becomes too dry after baking.)

Summary of processes: Chop 1 cup onion and 2¼ cups cooked chicken
Freeze in: 4-cup container
Serve with: Fresh Baked Asparagus (page 151)

Makes 4 servings

Heavenly Chicken

1 10-OUNCE PACKAGE FROZEN,
    CHOPPED SPINACH

White Sauce

½ CUP SLICED GREEN ONIONS

2 TABLESPOONS MARGARINE

2 TABLESPOONS ALL-PURPOSE FLOUR

1 CUP MILK (WHOLE, 2%, OR SKIM)

1 CUP SODA-CRACKER CRUMBS

1 CUP GRATED PARMESAN CHEESE

8 BONELESS CHICKEN BREAST HALVES,
    SKINNED, ABOUT 3¾ POUNDS

1 CUP COOKED, CUBED HAM

In a small saucepan, cook spinach according to package directions; drain well. In a medium saucepan, make White Sauce; sauté onions in margarine over low heat until tender, about 5 minutes. Stir in flour and add milk all at once. Cook over low heat, stirring constantly until bubbly. Boil and stir 1 minute more until smooth and thickened.

Combine cracker crumbs and cheese. Dip chicken breasts in soda-cracker crumbs to coat lightly. Arrange breast halves in a 13x9x2-inch baking dish. Seal leftover crumb mixture in a 1-quart bag.

Stir spinach and ham into White Sauce; spoon sauce over chicken breasts. Allow to cool and cover baking dish with foil, attaching bag of crumb mixture to side of dish.

To prepare for serving, thaw dish and bake covered in a preheated 350°F oven for 60 to 75 minutes. Uncover and sprinkle top with reserved soda-cracker crumbs. Bake 10 minutes more.

Summary of processes: Slice ½ cup green onions; crush 1 cup cracker crumbs; cut 1 cup ham into cubes
Freeze in: 13x9x2-inch baking dish; 1-quart bag
Serve with: Pineapple chunks and mandarin oranges sprinkled with shredded coconut, Cranberry Tea (page 144)
Note: This is practically a meal-in-one dish.

Makes 8 servings

Chinese Chicken Morsels

1 POUND BONELESS, SKINLESS CHICKEN BREASTS (2 CUPS)

Marinade
½ CUP LEMON JUICE
¼ CUP SOY SAUCE

¼ CUP DIJON MUSTARD
2 TEASPOONS VEGETABLE OIL
¼ TEASPOON CAYENNE PEPPER

1 CUP REGULAR, UNCOOKED RICE*

Cut chicken breasts (kitchen scissors work best) into 1-inch cubes. Make the Marinade combining the lemon juice, soy sauce, mustard, oil, and pepper. Put Marinade and chicken cubes in a 1-gallon bag and store in the freezer.

To prepare for serving, thaw chicken and remove from Marinade. Warm Marinade in a small saucepan. Place cubes about an inch apart on broiler pan treated with nonstick spray. Broil 4 to 5 inches from heat for 7 minutes, brushing with Marinade once. Turn chicken cubes and broil another 4 minutes. Meanwhile, prepare rice according to package directions. Heat remaining Marinade and serve over rice.

Summary of processes: Cut chicken into 1-inch cubes
Freeze in: 1-gallon bag
Serve with: Sliced, fresh tomatoes or tossed salad, Banana-Sauce Muffins (page 140)
Note: For a luncheon alternative, toss sautéed or broiled chicken morsels with mixed

salad greens, shredded carrots, cherry tomatoes, chopped, green bell pepper, sliced water chestnuts and croutons. Use your favorite low-calorie dressing.

Makes 4 to 5 servings

Poulet de France

1 12-OUNCE PACKAGE SEASONED BREAD STUFFING — 7-POUND BIRD SIZE (6 CUPS)
2 TABLESPOONS MELTED MARGARINE
2 CUPS CHICKEN BROTH
3 CUPS COOKED, CHOPPED CHICKEN
½ CUP FINELY CHOPPED ONION
¼ CUP MINCED CHIVES

½ CUP FINELY CHOPPED CELERY
½ CUP LIGHT MAYONNAISE
¾ TEASPOON SALT
2 EGGS
1½ CUPS MILK (WHOLE, 2%, OR SKIM)
1 10¾-OUNCE CAN CONDENSED CREAM OF MUSHROOM SOUP
½ CUP GRATED MILD CHEDDAR CHEESE

In a medium bowl, mix stuffing, melted margarine, and 1¼ cups of the broth. Mix chicken, the remaining broth, onions, chives, celery, mayonnaise, and salt in another bowl. Spread half the stuffing in a 13x9x2-inch baking dish treated with nonstick spray. Spread chicken mixture over stuffing. Cover with remaining stuffing. Whisk eggs, milk, and soup in a large bowl. Pour sauce evenly over stuffing. Cover dish with foil and freeze. Put cheese in a small freezer bag, and attach it to dish.

To prepare for serving, thaw grated cheese and chicken dish. Bake covered in a pre-heated 325°F oven for 30 minutes. Remove foil, sprinkle with cheese, and continue to bake uncovered for 10 minutes more.

Summary of processes: Chop 3 cups cooked chicken, ½ cup onions, and ½ cup celery; mince ¼ cup chives; grate ½ cup mild cheddar cheese
Freeze in: 13x9x2-inch baking dish; 1-quart bag
Serve with: Cooked frozen peas, Cranberry Sauce

Makes 8 servings

Meal-in-One Potatoes

½ POUND GROUND TURKEY

½ CUP FINELY CHOPPED ONION

1 TEASPOON MINCED GARLIC (1 CLOVE)

1 CUP CANNED, RED KIDNEY BEANS,
    DRAINED

1 8-OUNCE CAN TOMATO SAUCE

½ CUP CHILI SAUCE

1 TEASPOON DRIED OREGANO LEAVES

¼ TEASPOON SALT

4 MEDIUM BAKING POTATOES*

In a medium skillet, cook ground turkey, onion, and garlic until turkey is browned, about 10 to 15 minutes; add remaining ingredients except potatoes. Bring to a boil; reduce heat. Simmer 5 minutes. Cool and freeze in a 1-quart bag.

To serve, thaw filling. Wash and prick potatoes and bake in a preheated 400°F oven for 1 hour or until done. Heat filling until bubbly. Split tops of baked potatoes lengthwise and fluff pulp with a fork. Top each potato with filling.

Summary of processes: Chop ½ cup onion, mince 1 clove garlic
Freeze in: 1-quart bag
Serve with: Smoky Corn Chowder (page 149)

Makes 4 servings

Teriyaki Chicken

Marinade

½ CUP SOY SAUCE

½ CUP SUGAR

1½ TABLESPOONS RED WINE VINEGAR

2 TEASPOONS VEGETABLE OIL

1 SMALL MINCED GARLIC CLOVE

¾ TEASPOON GROUND GINGER

1 POUND BONELESS, SKINLESS
    CHICKEN BREASTS

1 CUP REGULAR, UNCOOKED RICE*

Mix soy sauce, sugar, vinegar, oil, garlic, and ginger to make the Marinade (reserve 2 tablespoons in a small bowl for Teriyaki Burgers). Freeze chicken in Marinade in a 1-gallon bag.

When preparing to serve, thaw chicken. Pour chicken and Marinade into a baking dish. Bake in a preheated 350°F oven for 35 minutes. Prepare rice according to package directions. Serve chicken over rice.

Summary of processes: Mince 1 clove garlic
Freeze in: 1-gallon bag
Serve with: Cooked French-cut green beans

Makes 4 servings

Mimi's Chicken Soup

1 SMALL ONION
2 OR 3 WHOLE CLOVES
1 CUP COOKED, DICED CHICKEN
2 QUARTS CHICKEN BROTH
½ TEASPOON SALT

1 TABLESPOON CHOPPED FRESH
  PARSLEY
3 SHREDDED CARROTS
½ CUP SLICED CELERY WITH LEAVES
1 8-OUNCE PACKAGE (USE HALF)
  TORTELLINI*

Peel and cut ends off onion; insert whole cloves into the onion. In a large pot, combine onion, chicken, broth, salt, parsley, carrots, and celery. Bring to a boil; reduce heat. Simmer uncovered for 1½ hours. Remove onion. Cool soup, put in container, and store in freezer.

To prepare for serving, thaw soup, put in large pot, and heat until bubbly. Add half a package tortellini, and boil 25 minutes more.

Summary of processes: Chop cooked chicken; shred 3 carrots; slice ½ cup celery; chop 1 tablespoon parsley
Freeze in: 8-cup container
Serve with: Swedish Rye Bread (page 139)

Makes 4 servings

Baked Herb Fish Fillets

4 FISH FILLETS (ABOUT 1¼ POUNDS
  ORANGE ROUGHY OR SOLE)*
½ CUP ITALIAN-FLAVORED BREAD
  CRUMBS
¼ CUP GRATED PARMESAN CHEESE

¼ TEASPOON GARLIC POWDER
¼ TEASPOON SALT
1 EGG WHITE, LIGHTLY BEATEN*
4 TO 5 NEW POTATOES*
1 SMALL LEMON*

Freeze fish fillets in a 1-gallon bag. Combine bread crumbs, Parmesan cheese, garlic powder, and salt in a 1-quart bag; attach to fish fillet package.

To prepare to serve, thaw fish and bread-crumb mixture. Lightly beat egg white and dip fillets in it. Put fillets one at a time in bag with bread-crumb mixture; make sure each is coated. Remove and arrange fillets in baking dish. Bake in preheated 375°F oven for about 15 minutes (until fish flakes easily) or in microwave oven on high for 4 to 5 minutes.

At the same time, prepare new potatoes. Peel a strip around the center of each potato. Heat 1 cup salted water to a boil; add potatoes. Cover, heat until boiling; reduce heat. Simmer tightly covered until tender, 30 to 35 minutes; drain. Serve potatoes with fish and lemon wedges.

Freeze in: 1-gallon and 1-quart bag
Serve with: Cooked zucchini

Makes 4 servings

Aztec Quiche

1¼ CUPS GRATED MONTEREY JACK
    CHEESE
¾ CUP GRATED MILD CHEDDAR CHEESE
1 9-INCH DEEP-DISH FROZEN PIE
    SHELL

1 4-OUNCE CAN DICED GREEN CHILIES
1 CUP HALF-AND-HALF
3 EGGS, BEATEN LIGHTLY
½ TEASPOON SALT
⅛ TEASPOON GROUND CUMIN

Spread Monterey Jack cheese and half of cheddar over bottom of pie shell. Sprinkle diced chilies over cheeses. In a bowl mix the half-and-half, eggs, and seasonings. Pour carefully into pie shell. Sprinkle with remaining cheddar. Cover pie with foil and freeze.

To prepare for serving, thaw pie and remove foil. Bake uncovered in a preheated 325°F oven for 40 to 50 minutes.

Summary of processes: Grate 1¼ cups Monterey Jack cheese and ¾ cup mild cheddar cheese
Freeze in: 9-inch oven-proof quiche or pie pan
Serve with: Fresh fruit salad, Cinnamon Logs (page 141)

Makes 6 to 8 servings

Baked Eggs

6 BREAD SLICES, CUBED
2 CUPS GRATED MILD CHEDDAR
    CHEESE
1 CUP COOKED, CUBED HAM
¼ CUP FINELY CHOPPED GREEN BELL
    PEPPER

½ CUP FINELY CHOPPED ONION
6 EGGS
3 CUPS MILK (WHOLE, 2%, OR SKIM)

Mix bread, cheese, ham, bell pepper, and onion; spread in a 13x9x2-inch baking dish treated with nonstick spray. Whisk eggs and milk and pour over top. Cover dish with foil and freeze.

To prepare for serving, thaw dish, and bake uncovered in a preheated 375°F oven for 45 minutes.

Summary of processes: Cut bread and ham into cubes; grate 2 cups mild cheddar cheese; chop ¼ cup green bell pepper, and ½ cup onion

Freeze in: 13x9x2-inch baking dish

Serve with: Frozen Fruit Medley (page 148)

Note: This dish is good with 6 slices cooked, crumbled bacon instead of ham. You can also make this dish the night before, refrigerate it, then bake and serve it the next morning. It's nice for company brunch.

Makes 8 to 10 servings

Teriyaki Burgers

2 TABLESPOONS TERIYAKI SAUCE (SEE   1 POUND LEAN GROUND BEEF
RECIPE FOR MARINADE IN   4 SANDWICH ROLLS*
TERIYAKI CHICKEN, PAGE 89)

Mix teriyaki sauce into ground beef; form four patties. Freeze patties in a 1-gallon freezer bag with a piece of waxed paper between each patty. Freeze sandwich rolls.

To serve, thaw rolls and patties. Grill or fry meat to desired pinkness. Serve on warmed sandwich rolls.

Freeze in: 1-gallon bag

Serve with: Potato salad, pickles, and black olives

Makes 4 servings

Bacon-Wrapped Burgers

4 STRIPS BACON

1 POUND LEAN GROUND BEEF

SALT

LEMON PEPPER

¼ CUP GRATED PARMESAN CHEESE

1 2-OUNCE CAN MUSHROOM STEMS AND
    PIECES, DRAINED

1 TABLESPOON MINCED ONION

2 TABLESPOONS FINELY CHOPPED
    GREEN BELL PEPPER

In a small skillet or microwave, cook bacon until limp, about 10 minutes. Drain bacon on paper towel. Pat ground beef on waxed paper into a 12x8x¼-inch rectangle. Sprinkle lightly with salt and lemon pepper. Top with Parmesan cheese.

Combine mushrooms, onion, and bell pepper; sprinkle evenly over ground beef. Roll ground beef like a jelly roll, starting from the longest side. Cut into 4, 1½-inch-wide slices. Wrap edge of each slice with a strip of bacon, securing with wooden picks. Freeze hamburgers with a piece of waxed paper between each patty. To serve, thaw patties; grill over medium coals 8 minutes. Turn and grill 8 more minutes or to desired doneness; Or broil hamburgers.

Summary of processes: Chop 2 tablespoons green bell pepper
Freeze in: 1-gallon bag
Serve with: Twice-Baked Potatoes Deluxe (page 150), Marinated Veggies (page 151)

Makes 4 servings

Ravioli Soup

1 POUND LEAN GROUND BEEF (2½ CUPS
    BROWNED MEAT)

¼ CUP SOFT BREAD CRUMBS

¼ CUP GRATED PARMESAN CHEESE

¾ TEASPOON ONION SALT

2 TEASPOONS MINCED GARLIC (2
    CLOVES)

1 TABLESPOON OLIVE OIL OR
    VEGETABLE OIL

1½ CUPS FINELY CHOPPED ONION

1 28-OUNCE CAN ITALIAN-STYLE OR

PLAIN CRUSHED TOMATOES IN
    PUREE

1 6-OUNCE CAN TOMATO PASTE

1 14½-OUNCE CAN BEEF BROTH OR
    BOUILLON

1 CUP WATER

½ TEASPOON SUGAR

½ TEASPOON DRIED BASIL LEAVES

¼ TEASPOON DRIED THYME LEAVES

¼ TEASPOON DRIED OREGANO LEAVES

¼ CUP CHOPPED FRESH PARSLEY

1 12-OUNCE PACKAGE PLAIN RAVIOLI WITHOUT SAUCE* (LOCATED IN THE FROZEN OR REFRIGERATED SECTION)	SALT GRATED PARMESAN CHEESE*

Cook the ground beef in a large pot until browned, about 15 minutes. Drain the fat. Combine remaining ingredients except frozen ravioli and additional Parmesan cheese. Bring soup to a boil; reduce heat. Cover and simmer 10 minutes, stirring occasionally. Cool, put in container, and freeze.

To prepare for serving, thaw soup base and put in a large pot. Bring to a boil; reduce heat. Simmer uncovered for at least 30 minutes, stirring occasionally. Thaw and cook ravioli according to package directions until just tender. Drain ravioli; add to soup. Salt to taste. Serve with Parmesan cheese.

Summary of processes: Mince 2 cloves garlic; chop 1¾ cup onion, ¼ cup parsley
Freeze in: 8-cup container
Serve with: Tossed green salad and Dawn's French Bread (page 138)

Makes 6 servings

Manicotti

1 8-OUNCE PACKAGE MANICOTTI	⅓ CUP GRATED PARMESAN CHEESE
1 TABLESPOON VEGETABLE OIL	1 TEASPOON SALT
1 15-OUNCE CARTON PART-SKIM RICOTTA CHEESE	¼ TEASPOON PEPPER
1 16-OUNCE CARTON LOW-FAT COTTAGE CHEESE	1 TABLESPOON CHOPPED FRESH PARSLEY
1 CUP GRATED MOZZARELLA CHEESE	2 EGGS 2½ CUPS SPAGHETTI SAUCE

Boil manicotti according to package directions, adding oil to water so they won't stick together. Meanwhile, mix ricotta cheese, cottage cheese, mozzarella, and Parmesan cheeses, salt, pepper, parsley, and eggs.

Drain manicotti; run cold water over it. Stuff each manicotti with cheese mixture. Place them in a 3-quart casserole, and pour sauce around stuffed manicotti. Cover dish with foil and freeze.

To prepare for serving, thaw dish. Bake covered in a preheated 350°F oven for 45 minutes. Uncover and bake for 15 minutes more.

Summary of processes: Grate 1 cup mozzarella cheese; chop 1 tablespoon parsley
Freeze in: 3-quart casserole
Serve with: Spinach salad

Makes 8 servings

Taco Pie

1½ POUNDS LEAN GROUND BEEF (3¾ CUPS BROWNED)
⅓ CUP FINELY CHOPPED ONION (¼ CUP SAUTÉED)
1 ENVELOPE TACO SEASONING MIX
1 4-OUNCE CAN DICED GREEN CHILIES, DRAINED
1 CUP MILK (WHOLE, 2%, OR SKIM)
1 CUP BISCUIT BAKING MIX

2 EGGS
1 CUP GRATED MILD CHEDDAR CHEESE
2 TOMATOES, SLICED*
1 8-OUNCE CARTON SOUR CREAM (OR PLAIN LOW-FAT YOGURT)*
1 CHOPPED TOMATO*
SHREDDED LETTUCE (ENOUGH TO GARNISH PIE)*

In a large skillet, cook and stir ground beef and onion until beef is brown, about 20 minutes; drain. Combine beef with taco seasoning mix and spread in a 10-inch pie plate. Sprinkle with chilies. Beat milk, biscuit baking mix, and eggs until smooth, 15 seconds on high in a blender or 1 minute with hand beater. Pour milk mixture over beef in pie plate. Cover plate with foil and freeze. Store 1-quart bag of grated cheese with pie.

To prepare for serving, thaw pie. Bake uncovered in a preheated 400°F oven for 35 minutes. Top with sliced tomatoes; sprinkle with cheese. Bake until golden brown, 8 to 10 minutes. Top with sour cream, chopped tomato, and shredded lettuce.

Summary of processes: Chop ⅓ cup onion; grate 1 cup cheddar cheese
Freeze in: 10-inch quiche or pie plate; 1-quart bag
Serve with: Guacamole dip with tortilla chips, fruit salad

Makes 6 to 8 servings

Joes to Go

1 POUND LEAN GROUND BEEF	½ CUP CHILI SAUCE
(3½ CUPS BROWNED)	¼ CUP BROWN SUGAR
¾ CUP FINELY CHOPPED ONION	1 TABLESPOON WHITE VINEGAR
(½ CUP SAUTÉED)	1 TABLESPOON PREPARED MUSTARD
1½ TEASPOONS GARLIC SALT	1 8-OUNCE CAN TOMATO SAUCE
⅛ TEASPOON PEPPER	6 HAMBURGER BUNS*

In a large skillet, cook and stir ground beef and onion until beef is brown, about 15 minutes; drain. Add garlic salt, pepper, chili sauce, brown sugar, white vinegar, mustard, and tomato sauce. Bring to a boil; reduce heat. Simmer uncovered 10 minutes, stirring occasionally. Cool and freeze. Keep with hamburger buns.

To prepare for serving, thaw hamburger sauce and buns. Heat sauce until bubbly and serve on warmed buns. Makes enough for 6 buns.

Summary of processes: Chop 1½ cups onion
Freeze in: 8-cup container
Serve with: Potato chips and carrot and celery sticks

Makes 6 servings

Winter Barley

1 POUND LEAN GROUND BEEF	1 TEASPOON WORCHESTERSHIRE SUACE
¼ CUP CELERY, CHOPPED	⅛ TEASPOON PEPPER
½ CUP ONION, CHOPPED	1 15-OUNCE CAN CHOPPED TOMATOES
¼ CUP GREEN PEPPER, CHOPPED	¾ CUP QUICK COOKING BARLEY
1¼ TEASPOON SALT	1½ CUPS WATER*
½ TEASPOON MARJORAM	

In a large saucepan, saute the beef, celery, onions, and green pepper until the beef is browned, about 15 minutes. Drain. Add the remaining ingredients, except the water, label and freeze.

When preparing to serve, thaw and add 1½ cups water. Simmer 30 minutes covered or until barley is tender.

Summary of processes: Chop ¼ cup celery, ½ cup onion, and ¼ cup green pepper
Freeze in: 1-gallon bag
Serve with: Cheesy-Herb Bread (page 135), pear halves with cottage cheese on top

Makes 6 servings

Cheesy Corn Casserole

1½ POUNDS LEAN GROUND BEEF (3¾ CUPS BROWNED)

1 17-OUNCE CAN CORN, DRAINED

2 EGGS, SLIGHTLY BEATEN

1 CUP SMALL-CURD COTTAGE CHEESE WITH CHIVES, DRAINED

1 TABLESPOON ALL-PURPOSE FLOUR

1 8-OUNCE CAN TOMATO SAUCE

½ TEASPOON MINCED GARLIC

¼ TEASPOON GROUND CINNAMON

1 CUP GRATED MOZZARELLA CHEESE*

In a large skillet, cook and stir ground beef until brown, about 20 minutes; drain the fat. Meanwhile, spread corn in bottom of an 8x8x2-inch baking dish. Combine eggs and cottage cheese; spread mixture over corn.

Stir flour into browned ground beef; cook 1 minute, stirring constantly. Add tomato sauce, garlic, and cinnamon to meat mixture and stir together. Layer meat mixture on top of cottage cheese and egg mixture. Cover dish with foil and freeze. Put mozzarella in 1-quart freezer bag; tape to baking dish.

To prepare for serving, thaw meat dish and cheese. Sprinkle cheese on top. Bake uncovered in a preheated 350°F oven for 30 minutes.

Summary of processes: Mince ½ teaspoon garlic; grate 1 cup mozzarella cheese
Freeze in: 8x8x2-inch baking dish; 1-quart bag
Serve with: Beets, Spicy Pumpkin Muffins (page 142)

Makes 6 servings

Ham Dinner Slices

2¾-INCH-THICK, COOKED HAM SLICES (FROM CENTER OF HAM)*
PREPARED MUSTARD*
BROWN SUGAR*

1 CUP MILK (ABOUT) (WHOLE, 2%, OR SKIM)*
4 MEDIUM BAKING POTATOES*

Freeze ham slices in 1-gallon bag.

To serve, thaw ham slices. Wash and prick potatoes and bake in a preheated 400°F oven for about 1 hour or until done. Place ham slices in a single layer in the bottom of an 8x8x2-inch baking dish treated with nonstick spray. Spread mustard on top of each slice; sprinkle brown sugar over mustard. Pour enough milk over ham slices to come halfway up their sides. Bake uncovered 45 minutes.

Freeze in: 1-gallon bag
Serve with: Cooked green beans, Hot Spiced Fruit (page 149)

Makes 4 servings

❏

CHAPTER 6

The Long Jump:
A One-Month Entrée Plan

❏

GROCERY SHOPPING AND STAPLES LISTS

An asterisk (*) after an item indicates that it should be stored until the day you cook the dish with which it is served. Mark those items with an X as a reminder that you will need them for an entrée.

When entrées require perishable foods to be refrigerated until served, you may want to prepare those dishes right away or buy the food the week you plan to make the dish. For example, fresh mushrooms would spoil by the end of a month.

For this one-month entrée plan, you will need these food items as well as the ones in the staples list that follows.

Grocery Shopping List

Canned Goods

> 1 bottle barbecue sauce (1 cup, your favorite)*
> 1 10¾-ounce can beef consommé
> 1 8-ounce bottle chili sauce
> 2 10¾-ounce cans condensed cream of chicken soup
> 4 10¾-ounce cans condensed cream of mushroom soup

THE LONG JUMP:
A ONE-MONTH ENTRÉE PLAN

SUN.	MON.	TUES.	WED.	THURS.	FRI.	SAT.
1 Eat Out Cooking Day!	**2** Split Pea Soup	**3** Salad Bowl Puff	**4** Jack Burgers	**5** Deborah's Sweet and Sour Chicken	**6** French Stew	**7** Shish Kebabs
8 Chicken and Rice Pilaf	**9** Grandma's Chili	**10** Crustless Spinach Quiche	**11** Grilled Ham Slices	**12** Green Chili Enchiladas	**13** Chicken à la King	**14** Sausage and Rice
15 Oriental Chicken	**16** Marinated Flank Steak	**17** Saucy Hot Dogs	**18** Sicilian Meat Roll	**19** Lasagna	**20** Oven Barbecued Chicken and Cheesy Biscuits	**21** Chicken Broccoli
22 Balkan Meatballs	**23** Baked Beans and Hamburger	**24** Jan's Sandwiches	**25** Bird's Nest Pie	**26** Chicken Tetrazzini	**27** French Dip	**28** Lemon Chicken
29 Grilled Fish	**30** Mexican Stroganoff					

1 4-ounce can diced green chilies

1 4-ounce can green chili salsa

1 16-ounce can whole green beans

1 15-ounce can kidney beans

1 8½-ounce can whole onions (or 8 ounces frozen small onions)

1 16-ounce can small peas

1 8-ounce, 3 4-ounce, and 1 2-ounce cans mushroom stems and pieces

1 2-ounce jar pimientos

1 31-ounce can pork and beans

2 8-ounce cans pineapple chunks (1*)

1 17-ounce bottle soy sauce (about 1⅛ cups)

3 16-ounce cans peeled tomatoes

1 12-ounce and 2 6-ounce cans tomato paste

1 15-ounce and 1 8-ounce cans tomato sauce

1 12-ounce can tomato juice

2 8-ounce cans sliced water chestnuts

Grains, Pasta, and Rice

1 10-ounce tube Hungry Jack Biscuits*

½ cup fine, dry bread crumbs

6 hot dog buns*

16 sandwich or onion rolls (8*)

4 hamburger buns*

1 8-ounce package lasagna noodles

1 5-ounce can chow mein noodles*

1 12-ounce and 1 8-ounce package wide egg noodles*

12 ounces dry, green split peas

1 32-ounce and 1 16-ounce package regular rice

1 16-ounce package spaghetti

8 to 12 flour tortillas

1 6¼-ounce package fast-cooking long grain and wild rice (use Uncle Ben's if available)

Dry Ingredients and Seasonings

1 package onion soup mix

1 package French's or Good Seasons French dip or brown gravy mix*

Frozen Foods

1¼ pounds frozen fish fillets (halibut, swordfish, or orange roughy)*

1 10-ounce package chopped broccoli

1 10-ounce package (use half) peas

1 10-ounce package chopped spinach

1 package puff pastry shells*

Dairy Products

¾ cup margarine or butter

13 eggs (2*)

1 16-ounce carton small-curd, low-fat cottage cheese

2 12-ounce cartons large-curd, low-fat cottage cheese

4 8-ounce cartons sour cream (or 1 carton 8-ounce plain low-fat yogurt for one of the cartons of sour cream)

1 8-ounce jar Cheez Whiz

12 ounces (3 cups) grated mild cheddar cheese

26 ounces Monterey Jack cheese (4 thin slices, 6 cups grated)

16 ounces sliced mozzarella cheese; 8 ounces shredded mozzarella cheese

7 ounces (about 1¾ cups) grated Parmesan cheese

1 cup half-and-half

1 quart milk (whole, 2%, or skim)

Meat and Poultry

2 pounds boneless, cubed, top sirloin steak

10 pounds lean ground beef (or turkey)

1⅓ pounds flank steak

2 pounds round steak

3 to 4 pounds sirloin tip or boneless beef rump roast

3 pounds beef stew meat

12½ pounds whole chickens or 10 pounds chicken breasts

4 boneless, skinless chicken breasts

3½ pounds chicken pieces (breasts, thighs, or drumsticks)

4 strips bacon

4 pounds cooked ham (1½ pounds cubed, ½ pound sliced thin, and 2 pounds from the center portion cut in 2¾-inch-thick dinner slices*)

½ pound ground turkey

2 pounds bulk Italian or turkey sausage

6 hot dogs or turkey franks*

1 2½-ounce package thin-sliced, corned-beef luncheon meat

Produce

4 carrots

1 bunch celery

8 cloves garlic (8 teaspoons minced)

1 bunch green onions

5 green bell peppers (4¼ cups chopped, ½*)

4 ounces whole fresh mushrooms*

4¼ pounds yellow onions

5 to 6 new potatoes
Half-pint box cherry tomatoes*

Staples List

Make sure you have the following staples on hand; add those you don't have to your shopping list.

allspice, ground
basil leaves, dried
bay leaves
biscuit baking mix (½ cup)
bread crumbs, soft (1 slice)
brown sugar (1⅛ cups)
catsup (¼ cup)
chicken bouillon cube (1)
chili powder
cinnamon, ground
cornstarch
croutons, seasoned (⅓ cup crushed)
curry powder
flour, all-purpose (about ¾ cup)
garlic powder
ginger, ground
lemon juice (⅓ cup)
light mayonnaise (about 1 cup)
minced onion
minute tapioca (¼ cup)
nonstick spray
nutmeg, ground
olive oil
onion powder
onion salt
oregano, dried
paprika
parsley flakes
pepper
prepared mustard
red wine (1 cup)
salt
sherry (¼ cup)
seasoned salt
sugar (½ cup plus ¾ teaspoon)

thyme leaves, dried
vegetable oil (about ¾ cup)
white vinegar (½ cup)
White wine (1 cup)
Worcestershire sauce

FREEZER CONTAINERS

The following list of freezer containers or baking dishes will be needed for the entrées. These are not the only containers you can use, but this list gives you an idea of the size and number of containers you'll need.

Heavy Aluminum Foil
> Jan's Sandwiches

5 1-Quart Freezer Bags
> Green Chili Enchiladas; Bird's Nest Pie; Grilled Fish; Crustless Spinach Quiche; Oven-Barbecued Chicken and Cheesy Biscuits

12 1-Gallon Freezer Bags
> Grilled Ham Slices; Balkan Meatballs; Jack Burgers; Sausage and Rice; Lemon Chicken; Chicken à la King; Oriental Chicken; Salad Bowl Puff; Marinated Flank Steak; Oven-Barbecued Chicken and Cheesy Biscuits; Sicilian Meat Roll

1 2-Cup Container
> Grandma's Chili for Saucy Hot Dogs

1 5-Cup Container
> Baked Beans and Hamburger

6 6-Cup Containers
> Split Pea Soup; Grandma's Chili; Chicken Tetrazzini (2); Shish Kebabs; Mexican Stroganoff

1 8-Cup Container
> Deborah's Sweet and Sour Chicken

1 14-Cup Container
> French Stew

1 11x7x1½-Inch Baking Dish
   Chicken and Rice Pilaf

3 13x9x2-Inch Baking Dishes
   Lasagna; Green Chili Enchiladas; Chicken Broccoli

2 10-Inch Quiche or Pie Plates
   Bird's Nest Pie; Crustless Spinach Quiche

THE DAY BEFORE COOKING DAY

1. Freeze hamburger buns, hot dog buns, puff pastry shells, frozen fish fillets, ham dinner slices, and all but 8 of the sandwich rolls.
2. Refrigerate ½ green bell pepper, whole fresh mushrooms, 1 whole onion, and store cherry tomatoes for Shish Kebabs.
3. Refrigerate 7½ pounds lean ground beef, sirloin tip or beef rump roast, 4 boneless chicken breasts, and 1 pound chicken pieces. Freeze remaining 2½ pounds chicken pieces for Oven Barbecued Chicken and Cheesy Biscuits in a 1-gallon bag marked with name of recipe.
4. Cover remaining whole chickens or breasts with at least 9 cups water in a large pot. Bring to a boil; reduce heat. Cover and simmer until thickest pieces are done, about 45 minutes to 1 hour. Cool chicken until ready to handle. Remove meat from bones and skin. Cut chicken into bite-size pieces with kitchen scissors, which are easier to use than a knife. Refrigerate chicken pieces in two plastic bags. (You will need 15½ cups diced, cooked chicken.)
5. Refrigerate 3 cups chicken broth; discard remaining broth or use for soup.
6. Set out appliances, bowls, canned goods, dry ingredients, freezer containers, and recipes.
7. Rinse split peas and soak them covered with cold water overnight.
8. Start French Stew in Crock-Pot (just before bed).

COOKING DAY ASSEMBLY

Make sure you've cleared the table and counters of unnecessary kitchenware to allow plenty of working room. It also helps to have fresh, damp washcloths and towels for wiping your hands and the cooking area. The day will go a lot more smoothly if you keep cleaning and organizing as you work.

Before you prepare a recipe, gather all the spices and ingredients in the assembly area to save time and steps. When you finish the recipe, remove unneeded items and wipe off the work space.

BEFORE ASSEMBLING DISHES

1. Cool and freeze French Stew. Wash out Crock-Pot.
2. Perform all chopping, crushing, grating, and slicing tasks.
    Bacon: Dice ¼ pound and 3 strips (put in separate dishes).
    Ham: Dice 2 cups, slice ½ pound thin, make thick dinner slices from the rest.
    Round steak: Cut into bite-size pieces.
    Onions: Chop 11⅔ cups fine; chop 1¾ cups coarsely for Shish Kebabs and Deborah's Sweet and Sour Chicken.
    Green onions: Chop onion bulbs only; discard green tops.
    Green bell peppers: Chop 3¼ cups; cut 1 cup in coarse pieces for Deborah's Sweet and Sour Chicken; save half of pepper for Shish Kebabs.
    Celery: Chop 1⅓ cups fine and 1 cup in coarse pieces; put in separate containers.
    Carrots: Peel and slice ¾ cup and 3 large; put in separate containers.
    Garlic: Mince 7 cloves (7 teaspoons).
    Mozzarella cheese: Slice all.
    Mild cheddar cheese: Grate all.
    Monterey Jack cheese: Cut 4 thin slices; grate remaining cheese.
    Crumbs: Crush ½ cup fine, dry bread crumbs; ¼ cup crouton crumbs; ¾ cup soft bread crumbs
3. Put ½ cup grated mild cheddar cheese in a 1-quart freezer bag; tape it to bag of chicken pieces for Oven Barbecued Chicken and Cheesy Biscuits.
4. Cook and stir 5¼ pounds ground beef in a large skillet until brown, about 30 minutes. Drain the fat and set aside.
5. In another large skillet, sauté 8½ cups onions in margarine until tender, about 15 minutes. Drain the margarine and set aside.
6. Spray pans or baking dishes you will need with nonstick spray (check list of freezer containers on page 104).
7. Skim and discard fat from chicken broth.

Assemble Beef Dishes

1. Assemble Grandma's Chili in Crock-Pot using 5 cups browned ground beef and ¾ cup sautéed onions.
2. Start baking sirloin tip or boneless beef rump roast for French Dip.
3. Make Lasagna using 2½ cups browned ground beef.

4. Start Mexican Stroganoff simmering in a large saucepan.
5. Assemble Baked Beans and Hamburger using 2 cups browned ground beef and ½ cup sautéed onions.
6. Prepare Balkan Meatballs.
7. Prepare Sicilian Meat Roll.
8. While meatballs are broiling, assemble Green Chili Enchiladas using 3¾ cups browned ground beef and ¾ cup sautéed onions.
9. Make Jack Burgers.
10. Freeze beef dishes.

Assemble Sausage Dishes

1. Cook 2 pounds of Italian or turkey sausage until brown, about 20 minutes; drain.
2. Break 1-pound package spaghetti in half, and cook as directed on package until al dente; drain. Toss half the noodles in ½ tablespoon oil to prevent noodles from sticking together; set aside for Chicken Tetrazzini.
3. Assemble Bird's Nest Pie, using remaining half of noodles.
4. Prepare Sausage and Rice.
5. Freeze sausage dishes.

Assemble Chicken Dishes

1. Complete Chicken Tetrazzini.
2. Prepare Deborah's Sweet and Sour Chicken.
3. Make Lemon Chicken.
4. Complete Chicken à la King.
5. Assemble Chicken Broccoli.
6. Prepare Chicken and Rice Pilaf.
7. Make Oriental Chicken.
8. Freeze chicken dishes.

Assemble Ham Dishes

1. Start Split Pea Soup simmering.
2. Assemble Salad Bowl Puff.
3. Complete Currant Ham Loaf.
4. Freeze ham dishes.

Assemble Miscellaneous Dishes

1. Assemble marinade for Grilled Fish.
2. Complete Marinated Flank Steak.

3. Prepare Shish Kebabs.
4. Complete Crustless Spinach Quiche.
5. Make Jan's Sandwiches.
6. Cool and freeze Grandma's Chili and Split Pea Soup.
7. Cool and slice sirloin tip or boneless beef rump roast for French Dip.
8. Freeze miscellaneous dishes.

RECIPES FOR THE ONE-MONTH ENTRÉE PLAN

Each recipe offers complete instructions on how to prepare the dish. Food items with an asterisk (*) won't be prepared until you serve the entrée. For recipes calling for oven baking, preheat oven for about 10 minutes.

"Summary of processes" gives a quick overview of foods that need to be chopped, diced, grated, or sliced. "Freeze in" tells what bags and containers will be needed to freeze each entrée. "Serve with" offers suggestions of foods to accompany the meal. Some of the recipes for those foods are included in Chapter 8; page numbers are indicated for easy reference. "Note" includes special instructions on how the entrée can be used in other ways.

French Stew

3 POUNDS BEEF STEW MEAT	1 16-OUNCE CAN PEELED TOMATOES
1 10¾-OUNCE CAN BEEF CONSOMMÉ	1 CUP WHITE WINE
3 LARGE PEELED AND SLICED CARROTS	¼ CUP MINUTE TAPIOCA
1 16-OUNCE CAN WHOLE GREEN BEANS, DRAINED	1 TABLESPOON BROWN SUGAR
	½ CUP FINE, DRY BREAD CRUMBS
1 8½-OUNCE CAN WHOLE ONIONS, DRAINED (OR 8 OUNCES FROZEN SMALL ONIONS, SEPARATED)	1 BAY LEAF
	1 TABLESPOON SALT
	¼ TEASPOON PEPPER
1 16-OUNCE CAN SMALL PEAS, DRAINED	

Mix all the ingredients in a large, covered pot. Bake in 250°F oven for 6 to 8 hours or in a large Crock-Pot 8 to 10 hours on low. Allow to cool, put in a 14-cup container, and freeze.

To prepare for serving, thaw stew and heat until bubbly in a large pot about 30 minutes.

Summary of processes: Peel and slice 3 large carrots
Freeze in: 14-cup container
Serve with: Frozen Fruit Medley (page 148) and Dawn's French Bread (page 138)
Note: This stew can be served over cooked wild rice. If you prefer potatoes, cook them and then add to stew when you serve it. (Note that potatoes don't freeze well.) You could also serve this stew on cooking day, freezing what's left over to serve later.

Makes 8 servings

Grandma's Chili

2 POUNDS LEAN GROUND BEEF (5 CUPS BROWNED)

1½ CUPS FINELY CHOPPED ONION (¾ CUP SAUTÉED)

1 CUP CHOPPED GREEN BELL PEPPER

1 TABLESPOON WORCESTERSHIRE SAUCE

¾ TEASPOON CHILI POWDER

¼ TEASPOON GROUND CINNAMON

⅛ TEASPOON GARLIC POWDER

SALT AND BLACK PEPPER TO TASTE

1 15-OUNCE CAN KIDNEY BEANS, DRAINED

1 16-OUNCE CAN PEELED TOMATOES

1 6-OUNCE CAN TOMATO PASTE

1 15-OUNCE CAN TOMATO SAUCE

Cook the ground beef with onions in a large saucepan until brown, about 20 minutes. Drain the fat and add remaining ingredients. Bring to a boil; reduce heat. Cover and simmer over low heat for 2 hours on a back burner or in a Crock-Pot on low for 6 hours, stirring occasionally. Cool, freeze in 1 6-cup container and 1 2-cup container for Saucy Hot Dogs.

To serve chili, thaw and heat in saucepan until hot and bubbly, about 30 minutes.

Summary of Processes: Chop 1½ cups onion, 1 cup green bell pepper
Freeze in: 6-cup container, Grandma's Chili; 2-cup container, Saucy Hot Dogs
Serve with: Cornbread, cottage cheese with pineapple chunks and mandarin orange slices
Note: This is a nice warm-up meal on a chilly day.

Makes 12 servings

French Dip

3 TO 4 POUNDS SIRLOIN TIP OR
    BONELESS BEEF RUMP ROAST
WORCESTERSHIRE SAUCE
8 SANDWICH ROLLS*

1 PACKET FRENCH'S OR FOOD SEASONS
    FRENCH DIP OR BROWN GRAVY
    MIX*

Place roast in roasting pan on a piece of heavy aluminum foil large enough to wrap meat in. Douse roast with Worcestershire sauce; seal meat in foil. Bake in preheated oven at 350°F for 4 to 5 hours on middle rack.

Remove roast from oven; allow it to sit 20 minutes before slicing. Save meat juices and put in a 1-gallon bag with sliced meat.

To serve, thaw sandwich rolls and roast and juices. Pour juices into a saucepan; add seasoning packet. Bring to a boil, reduce heat, and simmer according to package directions. Warm sandwich rolls and meat in a small amount of juice. Serve thin slices of roast in sandwich rolls with bowls of juice for dipping.

Freeze in: 1-gallon bag
Serve with: Waldorf salad, carrot strips

Makes 6 to 8 servings

Lasagna

1 POUND LEAN GROUND BEEF (2½ CUPS
    BROWNED)
1 TEASPOON MINCED GARLIC (1 CLOVE)
1 TABLESPOON PARSLEY FLAKES
1 TABLESPOON DRIED BASIL LEAVES
1½ TEASPOONS SALT
1 16-OUNCE CAN PEELED TOMATOES
1 12-OUNCE CAN TOMATO PASTE
1 8-OUNCE PACKAGE LASAGNA

2 12-OUNCE CARTONS LARGE CURD,
    LOW-FAT COTTAGE CHEESE
2 EGGS, BEATEN
½ TEASPOON PEPPER
2 TABLESPOONS PARSLEY FLAKES
½ CUP GRATED PARMESAN CHEESE
12 OUNCES SLICED MOZZARELLA
    CHEESE

In a large saucepan, mix browned ground beef, garlic, parsley, basil, salt, tomatoes, and tomato paste. Bring to a boil; reduce heat. Simmer uncovered for 30 minutes, stirring frequently.

Cook lasagna according to package directions until al dente; drain. Combine cottage cheese, eggs, pepper, parsley flakes, and Parmesan cheese. Grease a 13x9x2-inch baking dish. Place a layer of noodles in dish, spread half the cottage-cheese mixture over noodles, layer with half the mozzarella, top with half the sauce mixture. Repeat process, topping with noodles and covering with sauce. Wrap dish with foil and freeze.

To prepare for serving, thaw lasagna. Bake uncovered in a preheated 375°F oven for 30 to 40 minutes.

Summary of processes: Mince 1 clove garlic; slice 12 ounces mozzarella cheese
Freeze in: 13x9x2-inch baking dish
Serve with: Tossed green salad

Makes 8 servings

Mexican Stroganoff

2 POUNDS ROUND STEAK
1 CUP FINELY CHOPPED ONION
2 TEASPOONS MINCED GARLIC
    (2 CLOVES)
2 TABLESPOONS VEGETABLE OIL
1¼ CUPS RED WINE
½ CUP WATER
½ CUP CHILI SAUCE
1 TABLESPOON PAPRIKA
1 TABLESPOON CHILI POWDER

2 TEASPOONS SEASONED SALT
1 TEASPOON SOY SAUCE
1 8-OUNCE CAN MUSHROOM STEMS AND
    PIECES, DRAINED
1 12-OUNCE PACKAGE WIDE EGG
    NOODLES*
1 8-OUNCE CARTON (1 CUP) SOUR CREAM
    OR PLAIN LOW-FAT YOGURT*
3 TABLESPOONS ALL-PURPOSE FLOUR*

Cut steak into bite-size pieces. Cook and stir steak, onion, and garlic in oil in a large saucepan over medium heat until brown, about 15 to 20 minutes. Drain oil. Stir wine, water, chili sauce, paprika, chili powder, seasoned salt, soy sauce, and mushrooms into steak mixture. Bring to a boil; reduce heat. Cover and simmer 1 hour until meat is tender. Cool and store in freezer container.

To prepare for serving, thaw meat mixture and heat in saucepan until bubbly. Cook egg noodles according to package directions. Stir sour cream or plain low-fat yogurt and flour together; combine with meat mixture to make a stroganoff. Heat to a boil, stirring constantly. Reduce heat; simmer and stir about 1 minute. Serve Stroganoff over noodles.

Summary of processes: Cut steak in bite-size pieces; chop 1 cup onion; mince 2 cloves garlic
Freeze in: 6-cup container
Serve with: Tomatoes stuffed with guacamole, corn on the cob

Makes 6 to 8 servings

Baked Beans and Hamburger

3 STRIPS BACON, DICED

¾ POUND LEAN GROUND BEEF (2 CUPS BROWNED)

1¼ CUPS FINELY CHOPPED ONIONS (OR ½ CUP SAUTÉED)

1 31-OUNCE CAN PORK AND BEANS IN TOMATO SAUCE

1 8-OUNCE CAN TOMATO SAUCE

¼ CUP BROWN SUGAR

1 TABLESPOON PREPARED MUSTARD

¼ CUP CATSUP

SALT AND PEPPER TO TASTE

Cook bacon; drain on a paper towel, let cool, then dice. In a large skillet, cook the ground beef and sauté onions until tender, about 15 minutes. Drain the fat. Mix in bacon and remaining ingredients, put in container, and freeze.

To prepare for serving, thaw and bake uncovered in a large baking dish in preheated 350°F oven for 30 to 45 minutes.

Summary of processes: Dice 3 strips bacon; chop 1¼ cups onions
Freeze in: 5-cup container
Serve with: corn on the cob, tossed green salad

Makes 6 servings

Balkan Meatballs

1 EGG

¼ CUP MILK (WHOLE, 2%, OR SKIM)

⅓ CUP CRUSHED SEASONED CROUTONS

¾ TEASPOON SALT

¾ TEASPOON SUGAR

¼ TEASPOON GROUND GINGER

¼ TEASPOON GROUND NUTMEG

¼ TEASPOON GROUND ALLSPICE

1 POUND LEAN GROUND BEEF

½ POUND GROUND TURKEY

⅔ CUP FINELY CHOPPED ONION

1 8-OUNCE PACKAGE WIDE EGG
    NOODLES*

White Sauce

2 TABLESPOONS MARGARINE*

¼ CUP ALL-PURPOSE FLOUR*

2 CUPS MILK (WHOLE, 2%, OR SKIM)*

PARSLEY FOR GARNISH*

In a medium-size mixing bowl, beat egg with milk. Mix in crushed croutons, salt, sugar and spices. Add beef, turkey, and onion; mix thoroughly. Shape meat mixture into meatballs the size of walnuts. Place meatballs on a rimmed cookie sheet; broil until lightly browned, about 5 minutes. Cool; put meatballs in a 1-gallon bag, and freeze.

To prepare for serving, thaw meatballs. Cook noodles according to package directions. At the same time, make White Sauce in a large skillet. Melt margarine over low heat. Add flour, stirring constantly until mixture is smooth and bubbly. Gradually stir in milk. Heat to a boil over medium heat, stirring constantly. Boil and stir 1 minute until thick and smooth. Add meatballs to sauce. Bring to a boil; reduce heat. Cover pan; simmer 15 minutes, stirring occasionally. Serve meatballs and sauce over wide egg noodles. Chop parsley; sprinkle over top.

Summary of processes: Chop ⅔ cup onion

Freeze in: 1-gallon bag

Serve with: Cooked green beans, Mimi's Nutritious Bread (page 136)

Makes 4 servings

Sicilian Meat Roll

2 SLIGHTLY BEATEN EGGS

¾ CUP SOFT BREAD CRUMBS (1 SLICE)

½ CUP TOMATO JUICE

2 TABLESPOONS SNIPPED PARSLEY

½ TEASPOON DRIED OREGANO,
    CRUSHED

¼ TEASPOON SALT

¼ TEASPOON PEPPER

1 SMALL CLOVE GARLIC, MINCED

2 POUNDS LEAN GROUND BEEF

6 1-OUNCE THIN SLICES FULLY COOKED
    HAM

1¾ CUPS SHREDDED MOZZARELLA
    CHEESE (7 OUNCES)

In a large bowl combine eggs, bread crumbs, tomato juice, parsley, oregano, salt, pepper, and garlic. Stir in the ground beef, mixing well. On waxed paper, pat meat mixture into a 12x10-inch rectangle. Arrange ham slices atop meat, leaving a ¾-inch border around all edges. Sprinkle 1½ cups of the shredded mozzarella cheese over ham. Starting from a short end, carefully roll up meat, using waxed paper to lift; seal edges and ends. Seal in a 1-gallon freezer bag, label and freeze.

When thawed, place roll, seam side down, in a 13x9x2-inch baking pan. Bake in a 350°F oven for 1 hour and 15 minutes or until temperature registers 170°F and juices run clear. (Center of meat roll will be pink because of the ham.) Sprinkle remaining shredded mozzarella over top of roll. Return to the oven for 5 minutes or until cheese melts.

Summary of processes: Tear one slice soft bread into crumbs; mince 1 clove garlic; slice thin 6 ounces ham; shred 1¾ cups mozzarella cheese
Freeze in: 1-gallon bag
Serve with: Hot Spiced Fruit (page 149), Rolls

Makes 8 to 10 servings

Green Chili Enchiladas

1½ POUNDS LEAN GROUND BEEF
   (3¾ CUPS BROWNED MEAT)
1¼ CUPS FINELY CHOPPED ONION
   (¾ CUP SAUTÉED)
1 TABLESPOON CHILI POWDER
SALT AND PEPPER TO TASTE
2 CUPS GRATED MONTEREY JACK
   CHEESE (1 CUP*)

8 TO 12 FLOUR TORTILLAS
1 10¾-OUNCE CAN CONDENSED CREAM
   OF CHICKEN SOUP
1½ CUPS SOUR CREAM OR PLAIN LOW-
   FAT YOGURT
1 4-OUNCE CAN DICED, GREEN CHILIES

Cook the ground beef, and sauté onions until the meat is brown, about 15 minutes. Drain the fat. Combine with chili powder, salt and pepper. Reserve 1 cup cheese in a 1-quart freezer bag to use when serving. Spoon enough meat mixture and cheese on each tortilla to cover a third of it. Roll tortilla beginning at the filled edge. Place seam side down in a 13x9x2-inch baking dish treated with nonstick spray. When tortillas are completed, combine soup, sour cream, and green chilies to make a sauce; pour over tortillas. Cover dish with foil and freeze with bag of cheese taped to it.

To prepare for serving, thaw enchiladas and cheese. Bake uncovered in a preheated 375°F oven for 20 to 25 minutes. The last 10 minutes sprinkle the remaining cheese on top.

Summary of processes: Chop 1¼ cups onion; grate 3 cups Monterey Jack cheese
Freeze in: 1-quart bag; 13x9x2-inch baking dish
Serve with: Spanish rice, Salsa de Lentejas (page 150)

Makes 8 servings

Jack Burgers

1 POUND LEAN GROUND BEEF　　　　**4 THIN SLICES MONTEREY JACK CHEESE**
½ TEASPOON ONION SALT　　　　**4 HAMBURGER BUNS***
¼ TEASPOON FRESHLY GROUND BLACK
　　PEPPER

Form ground beef into 8 thin patties. Sprinkle onion salt and black pepper over them. Place a slice of cheese on 4 of the patties. Cover each with another patty, pinching to seal cheese inside. Freeze in a 1-gallon freezer bag with waxed paper between each set of patties.

To serve, thaw patties and buns. Grill or fry to desired doneness.

Summary of processes: Cut 4 slices Monterey Jack cheese
Freeze in: 1-gallon bag
Serve with: Pasta salad, root-beer floats

Makes 4 servings

Bird's Nest Pie

1 16-OUNCE PACKAGE SPAGHETTI (USE HALF)

2 EGGS, BEATEN

⅓ CUP GRATED PARMESAN CHEESE

½ CUP FINELY CHOPPED ONION (¼ CUP SAUTÉED)

2 TABLESPOONS MARGARINE OR BUTTER

1 8-OUNCE CARTON SOUR CREAM OR PLAIN LOW-FAT YOGURT (1 CUP)

1 POUND BULK ITALIAN OR TURKEY SAUSAGE (2½ CUPS BROWNED)

1 6-OUNCE CAN TOMATO PASTE

1 CUP WATER

4 OUNCES SLICED MOZZARELLA CHEESE

Break spaghetti in half and cook as directed on package until al dente; drain. While spaghetti is warm, combine with eggs and Parmesan cheese. Press spaghetti into bottom and up sides of a well-greased, 10-inch pie plate with a spoon. Sauté onion in margarine for 5 minutes, mix with sour cream or yogurt, and spread over crust.

At the same time, cook sausage in a large skillet until brown, about 15 minutes. Drain the fat. Stir in tomato paste and water. Bring to a boil; reduce heat. Simmer uncovered 10 minutes, stirring occasionally. Spoon over sour-cream mixture. Cover dish with foil and freeze. Put cheese slices in a 1-quart bag; attach to side of dish.

To prepare for serving, thaw pie and cheese. Bake pie uncovered in a preheated 350°F oven for 25 minutes. Arrange mozzarella slices on top; return pie to oven until cheese melts.

Summary of processes: Chop ½ cup onion; slice 4 ounces mozzarella cheese
Freeze in: 10-inch quiche or pie plate; 1-quart bag
Serve with: Strawberry gelatin, cooked fresh broccoli
Note: If you double this recipe, use 3 9-inch pie plates.

Makes 8 servings

Sausage and Rice

1 6¼-OUNCE BOX FAST-COOKING LONG
    GRAIN AND WILD RICE
1 POUND BULK ITALIAN OR TURKEY
    SAUSAGE
3 TABLESPOONS MARGARINE
1¼ CUPS FINELY CHOPPED ONION (1
    CUP SAUTÉED)
1 8-OUNCE CAN SLICED WATER
    CHESTNUTS, DRAINED

1 CUP CHOPPED, GREEN BELL PEPPER
1 CUP CHOPPED CELERY
1 4-OUNCE CAN MUSHROOMS STEMS
    AND PIECES
1 10¾-OUNCE CAN CREAM OF
    MUSHROOM SOUP
¾ TEASPOON SALT

Cook rice according to package directions. Cook sausage until brown, about 15 minutes. drain fat. Sauté onions in margarine until transparent, about 10 minutes. Combine rice, onions, sausage, and remaining ingredients; put in a 1-gallon bag and freeze.

To prepare for serving, thaw sausage and rice mixture. Put in a baking dish; bake uncovered in a preheated 350°F oven for 1 hour.

Summary of processes: Chop 1¼ cups onion, 1 cup green bell pepper, 1 cup celery
Freeze in: 1-gallon bag
Serve with: Cranberry Cream Salad (page 147), carrot and celery sticks
Note: This is quite spicy, so it isn't suitable for every palate.

Makes 6 servings

Chicken Tetrazzini

1 16-OUNCE PACKAGE (USE HALF)
    SPAGHETTI
1¼ CUPS FINELY CHOPPED ONION (1
    CUP SAUTÉED)
3 TABLESPOONS MARGARINE
1 CUP CHOPPED GREEN BELL PEPPER
5½ CUPS COOKED, DICED CHICKEN

4 CUPS GRATED MONTEREY JACK
    CHEESE
2 10¾-OUNCE CANS CREAM OF
    MUSHROOM SOUP
1 10¾-OUNCE SOUP CAN MILK (WHOLE,
    2%, OR SKIM)
SALT AND PEPPER TO TASTE

Break spaghetti in half and cook as directed on package until al dente; drain. Sauté onions in margarine until transparent, about 10 minutes. Thoroughly mix onions and remaining ingredients with spaghetti in a large bowl. Put spaghetti mixture in 2 6-cup containers and freeze.

To prepare for serving, thaw Tetrazzini and put in a baking dish. Bake uncovered in a preheated 350°F oven until bubbly, about 30 to 40 minutes.

Summary of processes: Dice 5½ cups cooked chicken; chop 1 cup green bell pepper, 1¼ cups onion; grate 4 cups Monterey Jack cheese

Freeze in: 2 6-cup containers

Serve with: Applesauce, Spring Cake (page 146)

Note: Serve half the Chicken Tetrazzini; take the other half to a family with a new baby or a housebound person. Include applesauce and cake.

Makes 12 servings

Deborah's Sweet and Sour Chicken

½ CUP SUGAR

3 TABLESPOONS CORNSTARCH

½ CUP WHITE VINEGAR

1 8-OUNCE CAN PINEAPPLE CHUNKS
   (RESERVE JUICE)

¼ CUP SOY SAUCE

½ TEASPOON SALT

1 TEASPOON MINCED GARLIC (1 CLOVE)

½ TEASPOON PAPRIKA

½ TEASPOON GROUND GINGER

1 CUP COARSELY CHOPPED CELERY

1 CUP COARSELY CHOPPED ONION

3 CUPS COOKED, DICED CHICKEN

1 CUP COARSELY CHOPPED GREEN
   BELL PEPPER

1 4-OUNCE CAN MUSHROOM STEMS AND
   PIECES, DRAINED

1 8-OUNCE CAN SLICED WATER
   CHESTNUTS, DRAINED

2 CUPS REGULAR, UNCOOKED RICE[*]

In a medium saucepan, combine sugar and cornstarch; stir in white vinegar, juice from pineapple chunks, soy sauce, salt, garlic, paprika, ginger, celery, and onion. Bring to a boil; reduce heat. Simmer, stirring constantly until thickened, about 20 minutes. Remove from heat. Stir in pineapple chunks, chicken, bell pepper, mushrooms, and water chestnuts. Put in an 8-cup container and freeze.

To prepare for serving, thaw chicken and put in a baking dish treated with nonstick spray. Bake uncovered in a preheated 350°F oven for 45 minutes. Prepare rice according to package directions. Serve chicken over rice.

Summary of processes: Mince 1 clove garlic; coarsely chop 1 cup each: onion, celery, bell pepper; dice 3 cups cooked chicken

Freeze in: 8-cup container

Serve with: Tossed green salad, dinner rolls

Note: If you want to fill the house with a good aroma, this is the dish! You can also substitute leftover cooked pork for the chicken.

Makes 8 servings

Lemon Chicken

1 TEASPOON DRIED THYME LEAVES

1 TEASPOON SALT

½ TEASPOON PEPPER

⅛ TEASPOON GARLIC POWDER

⅓ CUP LEMON JUICE

1 POUND CHICKEN PIECES

1 CUP REGULAR, UNCOOKED RICE*

Mix all the spices and lemon juice in a 1-gallon bag, add chicken pieces, and freeze. When thawed, preheat oven to 450°F. Arrange chicken skin-side down in a 8x8x2-inch baking dish treated with nonstick spray. Pour liquid over chicken. Bake 20 minutes. Turn chicken over, and baste it. Bake 15 to 20 minutes longer or until chicken is tender and no longer pink when cut along the bone. Prepare rice according to package directions. Serve chicken over rice.

Freeze in: 1-gallon bag
Serve with: Cooked fresh broccoli, Blueberry Pie (page 144)

Makes 4 servings

Chicken à la King

1 STRIP DICED BACON

½ CUP FINELY CHOPPED ONION

1 2-OUNCE CAN MUSHROOM STEMS AND
PIECES (RESERVE ¼ CUP LIQUID)

¼ CUP CHOPPED GREEN BELL PEPPER

1 TABLESPOON MARGARINE OR BUTTER

¼ CUP ALL-PURPOSE FLOUR

1 TEASPOON SALT

¼ TEASPOON PEPPER

1 CUP HALF-AND-HALF

⅔ CUP CHICKEN BROTH

1 TABLESPOON SHERRY

1 CUP COOKED, DICED CHICKEN

1 TABLESPOON PIMIENTOS

1 PACKAGE PUFF PASTRY SHELLS*

In a large saucepan, cook and stir bacon, onion, mushrooms and bell pepper in margarine over medium heat until vegetables are tender, about 15 minutes. Blend in flour, salt, and pepper. Cook over low heat, stirring constantly until well mixed.

Remove from heat. Stir in half-and-half, chicken broth, reserved mushroom liquid, and sherry. Heat to a boil, stirring constantly for 1 minute. Stir in chicken and pimientos. Allow chicken mixture to cool, put in a 1-gallon bag, and freeze.

To prepare for serving, thaw puff pastry shells and chicken mixture. Heat in a large saucepan until bubbly, stirring constantly, about 15 minutes. Serve in warmed puff pastry shells.

Summary of processes: Dice 1 strip bacon, 1 cup cooked chicken; chop ¼ cup onion, ¼ cup bell pepper
Freeze in: 1-gallon bag
Serve with: Fresh Baked Asparagus (page 151), red grapes or melon slices

Makes 4 to 5 servings

Chicken Broccoli

1 10-OUNCE PACKAGE FROZEN
    CHOPPED BROCCOLI
4 CUPS COOKED, DICED CHICKEN
1 10¾-OUNCE CAN CONDENSED CREAM
    OF CHICKEN SOUP

½ CUP LIGHT MAYONNAISE
1 4-OUNCE CAN MUSHROOM STEMS AND
    PIECES, DRAINED
¼ TEASPOON CURRY POWDER
¾ CUP GRATED PARMESAN CHEESE

Cook broccoli in boiling water according to package directions. Drain broccoli and spread in a 13x9x2-inch baking dish. Mix chicken, soup, mayonnaise, mushrooms, curry powder, and ½ cup Parmesan cheese in a medium bowl. Spread chicken mixture over broccoli. Sprinkle ¼ cup Parmesan cheese over top. Cover dish with foil and freeze.

To prepare for serving, thaw dish and bake covered in a preheated 350°F oven for 40 minutes. Remove foil, stir to bring colder food in center to the outside; bake 20 minutes more.

Summary of processes: Dice 4 cups cooked chicken
Freeze in: 13x9x2-inch baking dish
Serve with: Croissants, Cranberry Cream Salad (page 147)

Makes 6 servings

Chicken and Rice Pilaf

4 BONELESS, SKINLESS CHICKEN
    BREASTS
SALT, PEPPER, PAPRIKA TO TASTE
1¼ CUPS WATER OR CHICKEN BROTH
1 CUP REGULAR UNCOOKED RICE
½ ENVELOPE DRY ONION SOUP MIX
    (¼ CUP)

1 10¾-OUNCE CAN CONDENSED CREAM
    OF MUSHROOM SOUP
2 TABLESPOONS PIMIENTOS (½ OF A
    2-OUNCE JAR)

Sprinkle chicken breasts with salt, pepper, and paprika. Mix chicken broth, uncooked rice, onion soup mix, cream soup, and pimientos together; put in an 11x7x1½-inch baking dish. Place chicken breasts on top of rice mixture. Cover dish with foil and freeze.

To prepare for serving, thaw chicken dish. Bake uncovered in a preheated 375°F oven 1¼ hours or until chicken and rice are tender.

Freeze in: 11x7x1½-inch baking dish
Serve with: Marinated Veggies (page 151), dinner rolls

Makes 4 servings

Oriental Chicken

2 TABLESPOONS MARGARINE
2 TABLESPOONS ALL-PURPOSE FLOUR
1 CUP CHICKEN BROTH
1 CUP WATER
1 TABLESPOON SOY SAUCE

½ TEASPOON GARLIC POWDER
2 CUPS COOKED, DICED CHICKEN
⅛ TEASPOON PEPPER
1 5-OUNCE CAN CHOW MEIN NOODLES*

Melt margarine in a medium saucepan over low heat. Add flour and stir over medium heat until bubbly. Add broth, water, soy sauce, garlic powder, chicken, and pepper; simmer for 5 minutes. Cool and freeze in a 1-gallon bag.

To prepare for serving, thaw chicken. Heat in a pan until bubbly. Serve over chow mein noodles.

Summary of processes: Dice 2 cups cooked chicken
Freeze in: 1-gallon bag
Serve with: Egg rolls, fortune cookies

Makes 4 servings

Split Pea Soup

12 OUNCES DRY, GREEN SPLIT PEAS	⅓ CUP CHOPPED CELERY
3 CUPS WATER	¾ CUP PEELED AND SLICED CARROTS
½ POUND COOKED, CUBED HAM	1 CUP FINELY CHOPPED ONION
¾ TEASPOON ONION POWDER	1 BAY LEAF
⅛ TEASPOON DRIED THYME LEAVES	SALT TO TASTE
⅛ TEASPOON FRESHLY GROUND PEPPER	

Rinse split peas, soak them in cold water overnight; drain. Put peas with remaining ingredients in a large pot. Bring to a boil; reduce heat. Stirring occasionally, simmer about 2 hours until peas are tender and turn pasty. Cool and freeze in 6-cup container.

To serve, thaw soup and simmer until warmed through. If peas are too thick, add water to make consistency of thick soup.

Summary of processes: Soak split peas in water overnight; cut ham in cubes; peel and slice ¾ cup carrots; chop 1 cup onion, ¾ cup celery
Freeze in: 6-cup container
Serve with: Orange slices or canned peaches, cornbread

Makes 6 servings

Salad Bowl Puff

Ham Salad Filling	½ CUP GRATED MILD CHEDDAR CHEESE
1 10-OUNCE PACKAGE FROZEN PEAS	1 TABLESPOON MINCED ONION
(USE HALF)	¾ TEASPOON PREPARED MUSTARD
1 POUND COOKED, CUBED HAM (1 CUP)	⅓ CUP LIGHT MAYONNAISE*

Rinse peas under cold water to separate, but do not thaw; drain. Combine peas with ham, cheese, minced onion, and mustard. Put in a 1-gallon freezer bag and freeze. To prepare for serving, thaw ham salad filling, and make the following pastry:

*Pastry**	½ CUP BISCUIT-BAKING MIX
⅓ CUP PLUS 2 TABLESPOONS WATER	2 EGGS
2 TABLESPOONS MARGARINE	

Preheat oven to 400°F. Spray an 8-inch pie plate with nonstick spray. Heat water and margarine to a boil in a 2-quart saucepan. Add baking mix all at once, stirring vigorously over low heat until mixture forms a ball, about 1½ minutes. Remove from heat. Beat in eggs one at a time, and continue beating until smooth. Spread mixture in bottom of pie pan (not sides). Bake pastry uncovered until puffed and dry in center, about 35 to 40 minutes. Cool pastry. Just before serving, stir mayonnaise into cold ham mixture, fill pastry, and serve.

Summary of processes: Cut 1 pound ham into cubes; grate ½ cup cheddar cheese
Freeze in: 1-gallon bag
Serve with: Lemon gelatin made with shredded carrots and crushed pineapple

Makes 4 servings

Marinated Flank Steak

Marinade
½ CUP VEGETABLE OIL
¼ CUP SOY SAUCE
¼ CUP SHERRY

2 TEASPOONS WORCESTERSHIRE SAUCE
½ TEASPOON GROUND GINGER
1 TEASPOON MINCED GARLIC (1 CLOVE)
1⅓ POUNDS FLANK STEAK

Mix first six ingredients for Marinade. Put flank steak in a freezer bag, pour marinade over it, seal bag, and freeze.

To prepare for serving, thaw flank steak, remove from marinade, and barbecue 8 to 10 minutes per side; or set oven control to broil and/or 550°F. Broil steak 6 inches from heat until brown, turning once, about 6 minutes on one side and 4 minutes on the other. Cut steak across grain at slanted angle into thin slices.

Summary of processes: Mince 1 clove garlic
Freeze in: 1-gallon bag
Serve with: Twice-Baked Potatoes Deluxe (page 150), cooked zucchini

Shish Kebabs

2 POUNDS CUBED, BONELESS, TOP
  SIRLOIN STEAK
¾ CUP COARSELY CHOPPED ONION
1 4-OUNCE CAN GREEN CHILI SALSA
1½ TEASPOONS CHILI POWDER
1 TABLESPOON VEGETABLE OIL
¼ CUP DRY RED WINE
¼ TEASPOON SALT
PEPPER TO TASTE

½ GREEN BELL PEPPER*
1 ONION*
4 OUNCES WHOLE FRESH
  MUSHROOMS*
HALF-PINT BOX CHERRY TOMATOES*
½ OF 1 8-OUNCE CAN PINEAPPLE
  CHUNKS
1 CUP REGULAR, UNCOOKED RICE*

Combine cubed beef with chopped onion, salsa, chili powder, vegetable oil, red wine, salt, and pepper; put in a 6-cup container and freeze.

To prepare for serving, thaw meat mixture. Remove meat from marinade. Cut bell pepper and onion into thick pieces to put on a skewer. Alternate meat, vegetables, tomatoes, and pineapple on a skewer, and barbecue or broil. Baste with marinade while cooking. At the same time, prepare rice according to package directions. Serve Shish Kebabs with rice.

Summary of processes: Cut steak into cubes; Chop ½ bell pepper and 1½ cups onion into thick pieces
Freeze in: 6-cup container
Serve with: Corn on the cob and Spring Cake (page 146)
Note: Serve these the first week; otherwise, fresh vegetables will spoil.

Makes 4 servings

Grilled Fish

1¼ POUNDS FROZEN FISH FILLETS
  (HALIBUT, SWORDFISH OR
  ORANGE ROUGHY)*
5 TO 6 NEW POTATOES*

Marinade
½ CUP SOY SAUCE
¼ CUP WATER
¼ CHICKEN BOUILLON CUBE
2 TABLESPOONS OLIVE OIL
1 TABLESPOON BROWN SUGAR
2 TEASPOONS MINCED GARLIC
  (2 CLOVES)
½ TEASPOON GROUND GINGER

Freeze fish fillets and store new potatoes until you're ready to serve them. Whisk remaining ingredients in a small bowl to make Marinade. Freeze in a plastic bag taped to fish-fillet package.

To prepare for serving, thaw marinade and fish fillets. Marinate fish 30 minutes. Prepare new potatoes. Heat 1 cup salted water to a boil; add potatoes. Cover, heat until boiling; reduce heat. Simmer tightly covered until tender, 30 to 35 minutes; drain.

At the same time, remove fish from Marinade. Set oven control to broil and/or 550°F. Broil or grill fish for 10 minutes per inch of thickness or until fish flakes easily with a fork. Baste frequently with Marinade while cooking. If fish is more than 1-inch thick, turn once during cooking.

Summary of processes: Mince 2 garlic cloves
Freeze in: 1-quart bag taped to fish fillet package
Serve with: Tossed green salad

Makes 4 servings

Crustless Spinach Quiche

1 10-OUNCE PACKAGE FROZEN, CHOPPED SPINACH
1 BUNCH CHOPPED GREEN ONION BULBS (WITHOUT GREENS)
4 EGGS
1 16-OUNCE CARTON LOW-FAT COTTAGE CHEESE
2 CUPS GRATED, MILD CHEDDAR CHEESE
¼ CUP CROUTON CRUMBS*

Cook spinach according to package directions and squeeze to remove liquid. Combine spinach, green onions bulbs, eggs, cottage cheese, and cheddar cheese. Put into a quiche pan or 10-inch pie plate treated with nonstick spray. Cover with foil and freeze. Put crouton crumbs in a 1-quart bag and tape to pie plate.

To prepare for serving, thaw pie and crumbs. Bake uncovered in a preheated 325°F oven for 1 hour, adding crouton crumbs the last 15 minutes.

Summary of processes: Chop 1 bunch green onions; grate 2 cups cheddar cheese; crush croutons to make ¼ cup
Freeze in: 10-inch quiche pan or pie plate; 1-quart bag
Serve with: Fresh sliced tomatoes and Banana-Sauce Muffins (page 140)
Note: This dish is nice for a women's luncheon.

Makes 8 servings

Jan's Sandwiches

**1 2½-OUNCE PACKAGE THIN-SLICED,
CORNED-BEEF LUNCHEON MEAT
1 8-OUNCE JAR CHEEZ WHIZ**

**1 TABLESPOON MINCED ONION
2 TABLESPOONS LIGHT MAYONNAISE
8 SANDWICH OR ONION ROLLS**

Chop corned beef and mix with Cheez Whiz, onion, and mayonnaise. Spread filling on one bun; top with second bun. Wrap buns individually in foil and freeze.

To prepare for serving, thaw rolls and bake in foil in a preheated 350°F oven for 20 minutes.

Summary of processes: Chop corned beef
Freeze in: Foil wrap
Serve with: Chips, fresh fruit salad

Makes 8 servings

Saucy Hot Dogs

2 CUPS GRANDMA'S CHILI*
6 HOT DOG BUNS*
6 HOT DOGS OR TURKEY FRANKS*

This dish is not prepared until the day it is served.

Thaw the container of frozen chili that you reserved when preparing Grandma's Chili, the hot dogs, and buns. Cook hot dogs in a small amount of water or in the microwave according to package directions, drain, and cut lengthwise. Heat chili in a saucepan until bubbly. If desired, heat buns. Put hot dogs in buns, and smother with chili.

Freeze in: 2-cup container
Serve with: Corn chips, cottage cheese, sliced pineapple and mandarin oranges

Makes 6 servings

Grilled Ham

2 POUNDS CUT IN 2¾-INCH-THICK
    CENTER SLICES OF COOKED
    HAM*
1 CUP REGULAR, UNCOOKED RICE*

Glaze
¾ CUP BROWN SUGAR*
1 TABLESPOON PREPARED MUSTARD*
2 TEASPOONS WATER*
1 TABLESPOON VINEGAR OR LEMON
    JUICE*

Freeze ham slices in 1-gallon bag.

To serve, thaw ham slices. Prepare rice according to package directions. Mix remaining ingredients for glaze and spread over ham slices. Grill, broil, or barbeque ham slices 2 or 3 minutes per side, basting with sauce once per side.

Freeze in: 1-gallon bag
Serve with: Cinnamon Applesauce Salad (page 147), Twice-Baked Potatoes (page 150)

Makes 4 servings

Oven Barbecued Chicken and Cheesy Biscuits

2½ POUNDS CHICKEN PIECES*
½ CUP GRATED, MILD CHEDDAR
    CHEESE*

1 CUP BARBECUE SAUCE (FAVORITE)*
1 10-OUNCE TUBE HUNGRY JACK
    BISCUITS*

This dish is not prepared until the day it is served.

Freeze chicken in a 1-gallon bag and cheddar cheese in a 1-quart bag. Refrigerate sauce and biscuits until serving day.

To serve, thaw chicken and grated cheese. Preheat oven to 400°F. Treat a 13x9x2-inch baking dish with nonstick spray. Dip chicken pieces in barbecue sauce. Place them in pan, skin side up. Bake 40 to 45 minutes. Pile chicken pieces at one end of pan. Separate dough into 10 biscuits. Place them in the pan in drippings next to chicken. Sprinkle cheese over biscuits. Bake 15 to 20 minutes until biscuits are golden brown.

Summary of processes: Grate ½ cup cheddar cheese
Freeze in: 1-gallon and 1-quart bags
Serve with: Baked beans, cole slaw

Makes 5 servings

❑

CHAPTER 7

The Relay:
Table-Talk Questions

❑

Dinner-table conversation builds a sense of security and family identity in children, and helps us understand one another better as we tune into each other's day. In addition, studies of students who excel in school point to the benefit of directed conversation at a family dinner table, where each family member has his or her say, and then waits to hear the views of others.

Try some of these topics with your family, and with company, too.

TABLE-TALK QUESTIONS

1. Talk about one thing you started today and one thing you finished.
2. Is faster always better? Talk about when it is and when it isn't.
3. What worries you most?
4. Devise a family plan for evacuation of your home in case of fire.
5. Role play appropriate phone-answering and message-taking procedures.
6. Take a saying like "Start at the top and work down." Think of as many applications for it as you can.

7. Of what are you proudest?
8. If you could do anything you want for a career, what would it be?
9. Give a sincere compliment to the person on your right.
10. What responsibilities do you think parents have to their children?
11. Which of your friends' parents do you respect most and why?
12. What does it mean to be patriotic?
13. What would you most like to change about yourself?
14. Read off a list of state capitals. Going around the table, each person must try to match the state with the capital.
15. Start a story. After a few sentences pass to the next person to add to it and so on around the table.
16. (With young children) tell us about the picture you drew today.
17. (With young children) sing a song.
18. Discuss upcoming events or life-style changes that will affect your family, for example a new job, a new teacher or level in school, or the failing health of a grandparent.
19. What is one new thing you'd like to try?
20. Where is one place you would like to go?
21. How can you help people in your work?
22. What is your favorite smell or fragrance?
23. If you ran for a political office, what would it be? What would be your central campaign issue?
24. Tell about a time you broke a bone or were injured in some way.
25. What is your favorite song?
26. Let a child who plays an instrument give a brief concert: one child per night.
27. Mom and Dad tell what they worried about most and what they liked most when they were children.
28. Ask grandparents to reminisce about colorful characters in their families.
29. What are some of your family traditions?
30. Play family trivia: Where did Dad and Mom meet? How many second cousins do you have? What was the name of your first pet?
31. Talk about salaries. Give five or six examples of average earnings for various occupations. Do wages necessarily match the value or significance of the work done?
32. Share a memory that goes way, way back in your childhood.
33. What is the best thing that happened to you today? The worst thing?
34. What is the funniest thing that happened to you today?
35. Bring a newspaper clipping and discuss a character quality it exemplified, such as greed, courage, disregard for human life.
36. Tell a favorite memory from a wedding you attended.
37. Read excerpts from a letter recently written to the family.
38. What was the most interesting thing you learned today?

39. Tell about the main character in a book you're reading and the challenge he or she is facing.
40. What is the saddest movie or television show that you have watched?
41. If you could be a guest in anyone's home, whom would you choose?
42. Why do you like some people and dislike some others?
43. What would be your ideal vacation?
44. What is your favorite Christmas decoration? How did it become special to you?
45. Find and read a poem expressive of the current season.
46. Tell what someone said today that made you feel good about yourself.
47. If you were the opposite sex, what would be the hardest adjustment?
48. If you could change one physical feature, what would it be?
49. What is/was your nickname?
50. What characteristics do you see in you that came from your father/mother?
51. What qualities would you like to emulate from your parents/relatives?
52. Who is your favorite relative?
53. If you won the lottery, how would it change your life?
54. Tell about a time you were frightened.
55. Discuss what elements are included in a home mortgage. How does life insurance work?
56. Discuss what one should do if involved in a car accident.
57. Discuss how to shut off the water to the house.
58. Which holiday has the most meaning for you and why?
59. How do different types of music affect you?
60. What was your favorite childhood storybook? Why did you like it?
61. What is your favorite time of the day? Your favorite season?
62. Where do you want to be in 10 years?
63. What disability do you fear the most?
64. Tell about a figure in literature (or on television) who has impacted on your life.
65. Plan a pretend two-week vacation with one boat, four other people, and $10,000.
66. If you could live in a different century, what century would it be?
67. For what purpose were you born?
68. If you were invisible, who would you like to observe?
69. If you were invisible, what conversation would you like to hear?
70. Describe what you like best/least about the current season.
71. If you could change your name, what name would you chose and why?
72. If you could be a professional in sports, what sport would you chose?
73. Plan a favorite dinner party. What food would you serve? Who would you invite? Where would you have the party?
74. If you could own a store, what kind would it be?
75. If you had four eyes, where would you put the other two?

76. If you had one minute to grab something of value as your house burned, what would it be?

77. (With children) have one family member cover both eyes. Let the rest of the family help that person eat. Talk about how it would be to be blind.

78. (With children) put a cotton ball in each ear. Then cover the ears with a wool hat. Discuss what it would be like to be hearing-impaired.

79. If you could be a bird, which one would you chose and why?/ An animal?

80. (With children) what does a fireman (or other occupation) have in his/her pocket?

81. (With children) what is the hardest part of a teacher's job?

82. (With children) if you could be like any older person, who would you be like?

83. (With children) what would you do with your time if you didn't have a television?

84. (With children) what would you like to ask the president (or a historical figure)?

85. What would you like to ask your great-grandparents?

86. Each person chooses a letter of the alphabet. How many animals can you name beginning with your letter?

87. What do you like best/worst about being your age?

88. (With children) if you could fly, where would you go?

89. What is one of the best gifts you have ever given?

90. What is a favorite memory you have with your parent or sibling?

91. If you could give $1,000 away, to whom would you give it and why?

92. What is the nicest thing you've done recently for an elderly or disabled person?

93. What would you miss most without the sense of smell?

94. (With children) if your pet could talk, what would it say?

95. What would you miss most if you were stranded in the mountains for two weeks?

96. (With children) "Sticks and stones can break my bones. . . ." What words have hurt you?

97. If you were caught in a snowstorm, in the car, with a winter coat, what would you do to survive?

98. (With children) most uniforms include a hat. Which uniform hat do you like the most?

99. Why are churches usually built to be beautiful?

100. (With children) suppose you were "home alone." In your piggy bank you have $1.29. What would you do?

101. If you were all dressed up, what would you be wearing? Where would you like to be going, and with whom?

102. If you could buy any car, what would it be?

103. While walking on a beach, you find a newborn baby boy. He's having trouble breathing. What would you do?

104. Other than water, what do you think is the most common drink in the world?

105. "Over the river and through the woods to Grandmother's house we go." What landmarks do you remember passing on the way to your grandmother's house?
106. What are some objects that you particularly remember from a grandparent's house?
107. When you see the American flag, what do you think of?
108. Tell about your favorite birthday.
109. What is your favorite radio station and why?
110. Where is the most beautiful place you've ever been?
111. What was your favorite comic-book super hero?
112. Tell about a favorite memory of a grandparent.
113. If you have ever ridden on a train, tell about your ride.
114. What is your favorite flower? Your favorite tree?
115. Tell about a prize or an award you won.
116. If you were to live in another country for a year, what would you miss the most?
117. What foods do you most dislike?
118. Tell about a time when you were homesick.
119. Tell about a favorite teacher.

❏

Adapting the Game Plan: More Recipes to Enhance Meals

❏

BREADS

Cheesy-Herb Bread

½ CUP MARGARINE

1 ENVELOPE GOOD SEASONS CHEESE
    GARLIC SALAD DRESSING MIX (OR
    GARLIC AND HERB)

1½ CUPS MOZZARELLA CHEESE

1 LOAF FRENCH BREAD

Early in the day, set out these ingredients so the margarine and mozzarella cheese can soften to room temperature.

After you have placed the entrée in the oven, mix these ingredients together; slice loaf of French bread and spread with mixture. Place on cookie sheet and put in oven for the last 5 to 10 minutes of baking time of entrée.

You can also broil this loaf for 3 to 5 minutes or slice the French bread lengthwise into two halves and spread with the mixture. Put the two halves back together and wrap securely with foil. Freeze.

When ready to serve, bake at 400°F for 35 minutes. No need to thaw first. You can prepare several of these and have them available in your freezer for last-minute additions to any meal.

Mimi's Nutritious Bread

1 PACKAGE ACTIVE DRY YEAST
3 CUPS LUKEWARM WATER
1 CUP POWDERED MILK
½ CUP HONEY
4 CUPS WHOLE-WHEAT FLOUR (OR
   SUBSTITUTE 1 CUP WHEAT GERM
   FOR 1 CUP WHOLE WHEAT FLOUR)

1½ TABLESPOONS SALT
½ CUP VEGETABLE OIL
5 TO 6 CUPS ALL-PURPOSE FLOUR
MELTED BUTTER OR MARGARINE

In a large mixing bowl, dissolve yeast in lukewarm water. Add milk and honey and then 4 cups whole-wheat flour. Beat with a whisk until lumps disappear (it will be about as thick as cake batter). Cover bowl with a towel and let dough rise 60 minutes or until doubled in size.

Add salt and vegetable oil; beat in all-purpose flour, working all of it in until it's no longer sticky. Knead with a dough hook 3 to 4 minutes or 10 minutes by hand, until dough is smooth. Put dough in a large, greased bowl, turning it once so it's greased on the top and bottom. Cover bowl with a towel and let dough rise 50 minutes or until doubled in size.

Punch dough down and let it rise 40 more minutes or until doubled in size. Divide dough in half, and shape into 2 large, smooth loaves. Grease pans with vegetable shortening, and put loaves in pans. Cover pans with a towel, and let dough rise 30 minutes or until doubled. Set timer for 15 minutes to remind yourself to preheat oven to 350°F. Bake 1 hour. Remove loaves from oven; brush tops with melted butter or margarine.

Makes 2 loaves

For the two recipes that follow, use Mimi's Nutritious Bread ingredient list.

Dinner Rolls

Divide dough in half, making one half into a loaf. Make dinner rolls out of the other half by rolling dough into a long tube about 2 inches thick. Cut the tube at 2-inch intervals; roll each piece into a round ball. Bake rolls on a cookie sheet in a preheated oven at 350°F for 25 to 30 minutes. Rub a cube of butter over the tops of warm rolls.

Cheddar-Beef Rolls

Form dough into balls according to the Dinner Roll directions; then flatten balls into circles about the size of your palm. Fold each circle of dough around a small wedge of cheddar cheese and 2 tablespoons browned ground beef. Preheat oven to 350°F. Bake sealed-side down on a cookie sheet 25 to 30 minutes. Put barbecue sauce in individual serving dishes. Dip rolls in sauce. These are great for lunch.

Portuguese Sweet Bread

2 PACKAGES ACTIVE DRY YEAST	4 EGGS
1⅔ CUPS WARM WATER	1 TABLESPOON FINELY SHREDDED
1 CUP DRY INSTANT POTATO FLAKES	LEMON OR ORANGE PEEL, OR ½
1 CUP SUGAR	TABLESPOON EACH
6 TABLESPOONS MELTED MARGARINE	¾ CUP RAISINS
OR BUTTER	¾ CUP GOLDEN RAISINS
2 TEASPOONS SALT	7½ CUPS ALL-PURPOSE FLOUR

In a large mixing bowl, soften yeast in warm water. Mix in potato flakes, sugar, melted margarine, salt, eggs, peel, and raisins. Add flour until dough is no longer sticky, about 7½ cups. Knead with dough hook 2 to 3 minutes or by hand 10 minutes, until smooth. Put dough in a large, greased bowl, turning it once so it's greased on the top and bottom. Cover bowl with a towel.

Let dough rise 1½ hours or until doubled in size. Punch it down and let it rise 10 minutes more. Divide dough into 3 large, round loaves or 4 smaller ones; place them on a greased cookie sheet with space between them. You can also braid the dough or form it into any shape.

Cover dough with a towel and allow it to rise until *almost* doubled in size, about 45 minutes. Bake loaves in a preheated oven at 350°F for 35 to 40 minutes, depending on number of loaves. Cover them with foil after the first 20 minutes so they won't get too brown.

Note: This bread makes great toast. We enjoy giving these festive loaves to our neighbors for Christmas.

Makes 3 or 4 loaves

Dawn's French Bread

1 **PACKAGE DRY YEAST**
3 **CUPS WARM WATER**
3 **TABLESPOONS SUGAR**

1½ **TABLESPOONS SALT**
7½ **TO 8 CUPS FLOUR**

In a large mixing bowl, dissolve yeast in 1 cup of the warm water. Add sugar and salt; let stand 5 minutes. Stir in the remaining 2 cups of water and 3 of the cups of flour, beating with the paddle on a heavy-duty mixer or by hand with a wooden spoon.

Add remaining flour a cup at a time. Knead with dough hook 4 to 6 minutes or 8 to 10 minutes by hand, until the dough feels smooth and elastic. Cover with a towel; let dough rise until almost tripled in size. Or make dough early in the morning and let it rise all day. Shape dough into 4 baguettes (long, slender loaves). Let loaves rise about 45 minutes until doubled in size. Preheat oven to 450°F. Bake for 15 minutes. Reduce temperature to 350°.; bake for 30 more minutes or until golden brown.

Note: Freeze each baked loaf in foil. To reheat, loosen one end of foil and heat loaf at 375°F until hot and crisp—about 20 minutes. You may also want to use this dough for Pizza Roll-Ups or Veggie Pizza instead of commercial frozen dough.

Makes 4 loaves

Swedish Rye Bread

2 PACKAGES DRY YEAST

1 TEASPOON PLUS ¼ CUP SUGAR

9½ CUPS ALL-PURPOSE FLOUR

2 CUPS WARM WATER

2 CUPS MILK (WHOLE, 2%, OR SKIM)

5 TABLESPOONS SOFT MARGARINE

½ CUP BROWN SUGAR

½ CUP MOLASSES

1 TABLESPOON SALT

1¼ TEASPOONS ANISE SEED

2 TEASPOONS CARAWAY SEED

3 CUPS RYE FLOUR

3 TABLESPOONS DARK CORN SYRUP

Combine yeast, 1 teaspoon sugar, 1½ cups of the all-purpose flour, and 1 cup of the warm water in a small bowl. Cover and let rise about 30 minutes.

In a small saucepan, scald 2 cups milk in remaining cup of warm water. In a large bowl, combine margarine, brown sugar, ¼ cup white sugar, molasses, salt, anise seed, caraway seed, 1 more cup of the all-purpose flour, rye flour, and dark corn syrup. Stir scalded milk into this mixture. Let it cool until it's warm to the touch. Stir in yeast mixture. Gradually stir in 3 cups all-purpose flour until a ball forms. Then turn dough onto a hard surface and gradually mix in 4 more cups flour, kneading dough 8 to 10 minutes until it's smooth and elastic. Put dough into a greased bowl covered with a towel; let rise until doubled in size, about 50 minutes.

Divide dough to make 3 or 4 loaves. Put them in greased loaf pans or shape dough into 5 or 6 small loaves and bake them on ungreased cookie sheets.

Let loaves rise about 45 minutes, then bake at 325°F. for about 40 to 50 minutes, depending on size and number of loaves. Rub a butter cube over tops of the warm loaves. Remove them from pans immediately and cool.

Note: These loaves are excellent as an alternative to cookies and fudge for Christmas gifts.

Makes 3 to 4 regular loaves or 5 to 6 small loaves

Banana-Sauce Muffins

1¼ CUP FLOUR

1½ CUP QUICK-COOKING OATMEAL

⅓ CUP SUGAR

1 TEASPOON BAKING POWDER

¾ TEASPOON BAKING SODA

½ TEASPOON SALT

1 RIPE BANANA, MASHED

APPLESAUCE

1 EGG

⅓ CUP DARK BROWN SUGAR

⅓ CUP MILK (WHOLE, 2%, OR SKIM)

¼ CUP VEGETABLE OIL

1 TEASPOON VANILLA

In mixing bowl, combine flour, oatmeal, sugar, baking powder, baking soda, and salt. Place mashed banana in 1-cup measure; add enough applesauce to make 1 cup. Combine banana-applesauce mixture with egg, brown sugar, milk, oil, and vanilla. Add liquid ingredients to dry ingredients all at once; stir just until moistened. Spoon into paper-lined muffin pans. Bake in 350°F oven for 15 to 18 minutes.

These muffins freeze well. Cool muffins thoroughly and wrap each muffin in plastic wrap before placing them into a freezer bag.

Makes 1 dozen

Apple-Date Freezer Coffee Cake

Topping

⅔ CUP FIRMLY PACKED DARK BROWN
    SUGAR

½ CUP CHOPPED WALNUTS OR PECANS

1 TEASPOON CINNAMON

2 TABLESPOONS BUTTER OR
    MARGARINE, MELTED

Cake ingredients

½ CUP BUTTER OR MARGARINE,
    SOFTENED

¾ CUP SUGAR

2 EGGS

1 CUP SOUR CREAM OR PLAIN YOGURT

1 TEASPOON VANILLA

2 CUPS FLOUR

1 TEASPOON BAKING POWDER

1 TEASPOON BAKING SODA

½ TEASPOON SALT

1 LARGE GOLDEN DELICIOUS APPLE,
    CORED AND COARSELY GRATED
    (USE MINI FOOD PROCESSOR)

½ CUP CHOPPED DATES

Grease a 9x9-inch baking pan. Combine topping ingredients in small bowl; set aside. In large bowl, with mixer at medium speed, beat ½ cup butter or margarine with sugar until light and fluffy. Add eggs, sour cream (or yogurt), and vanilla; beat until well blended. In separate bowl, combine flour, baking powder, baking soda, and salt. Stir dry ingredients into creamed mixture; blend. Stir in Golden Delicious apple and dates. Pour into prepared pan. Sprinkle evenly with topping. Wrap tightly with foil and freeze.

About 1½ hours before serving, preheat oven to 350°F. Bake frozen coffee cake, uncovered, 60 to 65 minutes or until toothpick inserted in center comes out clean. Serve warm or cool in pan for serving later.

Makes 9 servings

Cinnamon Logs

2 EGG YOLKS
1¾ CUPS SUGAR
2 8-OUNCE PACKAGES CREAM CHEESE, SOFTENED

3 LOAVES PEPPERIDGE FARM SANDWICH BREAD (OR OTHER VERY FIRM, THIN-SLICED WHITE BREAD)
1 POUND (4 STICKS) MARGARINE
4 TEASPOONS GROUND CINNAMON

Beat egg yolks and ½ cup sugar together; stir in cream cheese until smooth. Trim crusts from bread; use a rolling pin to flatten each slice.

Spread cheese mixture on a slice of bread; top with another slice to make a sandwich. Do the same with the remaining bread slices. Cut each sandwich lengthwise into 4 logs.

Melt margarine. Mix cinnamon and remaining 1¼ cups sugar in a bowl. Dip each log in melted margarine and then in cinnamon sugar. Place on rimmed cookie sheets. Bake in a preheated 400°F oven for 10 minutes.

Note: Before baking logs, freeze them on rimmed cookie sheets; then put them in freezer bags. To serve, remove as many logs as you need from the bag. Put frozen logs on a cookie sheet or flat baking dish and bake in a preheated 400°F oven for 10 minutes.

Makes 80 to 100 logs

Spicy Pumpkin Muffins

1½ CUPS ALL-PURPOSE FLOUR

½ CUP SUGAR

2 TEASPOONS BAKING POWDER

¾ TEASPOON SALT

1 TEASPOON GROUND CINNAMON

½ TEASPOON GROUND GINGER

¼ TEASPOON GROUND CLOVES

½ CUP RAISINS

1 EGG

½ CUP MILK (WHOLE, 2%, OR SKIM)

½ CUP CANNED PUMPKIN

¼ CUP VEGETABLE OIL

Topping

2½ TEASPOONS SUGAR

½ TEASPOON GROUND CINNAMON

Stir flour, sugar, baking powder, salt, and spices in a large mixing bowl until well combined. Then mix in raisins. Beat egg, milk, pumpkin, and salad oil in a smaller bowl. Pour pumpkin mixture into flour and spices, stirring only until combined. Fill lightly greased muffin cups ⅔ full. Mix sugar and cinnamon; sprinkle on muffins. Bake in a preheated 400°F oven 20 to 25 minutes or until nicely browned. Serve warm.

Makes 12 muffins

Auntie Teeto's Waffles

2 CUPS ALL-PURPOSE FLOUR (OR
    SUBSTITUTE ½ CUP WHOLE
    WHEAT OR BUCKWHEAT FLOUR
    FOR ½ CUP OF THE ALL-PURPOSE
    FLOUR)

1 TEASPOON BAKING SODA

1 TEASPOON SALT

2 EGGS

1½ CUPS BUTTERMILK

2 TABLESPOONS VEGETABLE OIL

MAPLE SYRUP (OPT.)

Preheat waffle iron, and spray with nonstick spray. Sift together flour, baking soda, and salt. In a medium bowl, lightly beat eggs; stir in buttermilk and vegetable oil. Add liquid ingredients to flour mixture, stirring just to moisten. Pour a circle of batter about 5 inches in diameter into the center of a waffle iron. Bake according to waffle iron's instructions or until steaming stops, about 5 minutes. Serve with warmed maple syrup.

Note: This recipe was given to Mimi by her ninety-four-year-old aunt, who used an equally old waffle iron. These waffles are great for Sunday supper for college students. Serve waffles with sausage and hot chocolate.

Makes 6 servings

Good Day Granola

8 CUPS ROLLED OATS (NOT INSTANT)	¾ CUP CHOPPED WALNUTS
1¼ CUPS FIRMLY PACKED BROWN SUGAR	½ CUP RAW SUNFLOWER SEEDS
1½ CUPS UNPROCESSED BRAN	½ CUP VEGETABLE OIL
1½ CUPS NATURAL WHEAT GERM (NOT TOASTED OR HONEYED)	¾ CUP HONEY
	2 TEASPOONS VANILLA
	2 CUPS RAISINS

Stir oats, brown sugar, bran, wheat germ, walnuts, and sunflower seeds in a large bowl. Put vegetable oil, honey, and vanilla in a small saucepan; heat, stirring until bubbly. Pour liquid over dry ingredients, mixing thoroughly.

Divide oat mixture evenly and spread on two rimmed cookie sheets. Bake in a preheated oven at 325°F for 15 to 20 minutes, stirring once to keep granola evenly browned. While it cools, stir mixture several times to keep it from sticking together. When completely cool, add raisins. Store in an airtight container.

Note: This granola keeps for weeks and is yummy for breakfast or snacks.

Makes about 16 cups

BEVERAGES

Orange Spiced Tea

2 CUPS POWDERED ORANGE DRINK MIX	1 TEASPOON GROUND CLOVES
¾ CUP INSTANT TEA MIX	1 2-QUART PACKAGE PRESWEETENED DRY LEMONADE MIX
1 TEASPOON GROUND CINNAMON	

Mix all the ingredients together. To serve, stir 2 heaping teaspoons of the mix into an 8-ounce mug of hot water or a 10-ounce glass of cold water. This drink is great hot or cold.

Cranberry Tea

1 CUP CRANBERRY JUICE

3 CUPS PREPARED ICED TEA

3 TABLESPOONS LEMON JUICE

¼ CUP SUGAR

Combine all ingredients. Serve hot or cold.

Makes 1 quart

DESSERTS

Blueberry Pie

1 10-OUNCE JAR CURRANT JELLY

1 PINT FRESH BLUEBERRIES

1 GRAHAM CRACKER CRUST, BAKED
    (RECIPE FOLLOWS)

1 CUP SOUR CREAM (OR WHIPPED
    TOPPING FOR A SWEETER PIE)

Melt jelly in a saucepan over low heat. Add blueberries and stir. Pour into baked graham cracker crust. Spread sour cream on top, and refrigerate overnight.

Note: This pie is so easy and so good!

Makes 6 to 8 servings

Graham Cracker Crust

1½ CUPS CRUSHED GRAHAM CRACKERS

3 TABLESPOONS SUGAR

⅓ CUP MELTED MARGARINE OR BUTTER

Crush graham crackers in a plastic bag, using a rolling pin. Mix crumbs with sugar and melted margarine. Press crumb mixture against bottom and sides of a 9-inch pie pan. Bake in a preheated oven at 350°F for 10 minutes.

Makes 6 to 8 servings

Blueberry Peach Fruit Crisp

This is a great winter dessert. You make it all the day you want to serve it, but you can freeze/store all the ingredients well in advance.

1 16-OUNCE BAG FROZEN PEACH SLICES (DEFROSTED)

1 10-OUNCE BOX FROZEN BLUEBERRIES (DEFROSTED)

1 CUP FROZEN APPLE-JUICE CONCENTRATE (DEFROSTED)

¼ CUP INSTANT TAPIOCA

¾ TEASPOON CINNAMON

Topping

1¾ CUPS FAT-FREE GRANOLA (OR LOW-FAT GRANOLA), WITHOUT FRUIT ADDED

2 TABLESPOONS FROZEN APPLE-JUICE CONCENTRATE (DEFROSTED)

Preheat oven to 350°F. In 8-inch square ovenproof glass baking dish, stir together peaches, blueberries, apple-juice concentrate, tapioca, and cinnamon.

For topping, grind granola with apple-juice concentrate in food processor or blender for about 2 minutes. Spoon granola topping over fruit mixture. Bake covered at 350°F for 30 minutes; remove cover and continue to bake additional 10 minutes until topping is lightly browned and fruit is tender. Cool on wire rack for 15 minutes. Serve warm or cold. Great served warm with vanilla frozen yogurt.

Makes 9 servings

Low-Calorie Chocolate Cake

3 CUPS ALL-PURPOSE FLOUR

½ CUP SUGAR

⅓ CUP UNSWEETENED COCOA POWDER

2 TEASPOONS BAKING SODA

1 TEASPOON SALT

2 CUPS WATER

2 TABLESPOONS WHITE VINEGAR

4 TEASPOONS CHOCOLATE SYRUP

2 TEASPOONS VANILLA

⅓ CUP SUGAR

¾ CUP MARGARINE

2 TEASPOONS VEGETABLE OIL

Preheat oven to 350°F. Mix flour, sugar, cocoa powder, baking soda, and salt; set aside. Mix water, vinegar, syrup, and vanilla in a separate bowl; set aside. Cream sugar, margarine, and vegetable oil in a large mixing bowl until fluffy. Alternate adding the dry and wet mixtures to the sugar and vegetable oil, beating well. Spray a Bundt pan with nonstick spray.

Pour batter into Bundt pan, and bake 40 minutes. Serve with whipped cream or whipped topping if desired.

Makes 12 to 16 servings

Spring Cake

½ CUP MARGARINE	1 TEASPOON GROUND CINNAMON
½ CUP VEGETABLE OIL	2 CUPS ALL-PURPOSE FLOUR
¼ CUP UNSWEETENED COCOA POWDER	2 CUPS SUGAR
1 CUP WATER	2 EGGS
1 TEASPOON BAKING SODA	1 TEASPOON VANILLA
½ CUP BUTTERMILK	½ TEASPOON SALT

Preheat oven to 400°F. Bring margarine, vegetable oil, cocoa powder, and water to a boil in a large saucepan, stirring constantly. Remove pan from stove. Stir baking soda into buttermilk and add it to the cocoa mixture along with cinnamon, flour, sugar, eggs, vanilla, and salt. Stir until well mixed. Pour batter into a greased and floured 13x9x2-inch baking pan. Bake for 20 to 25 minutes. Ice with Cocoa Frosting (recipe follows) while cake is still warm.

Makes 12 servings

Cocoa Frosting

½ CUP MARGARINE	16 OUNCES POWDERED SUGAR
⅓ CUP BUTTERMILK	1 TEASPOON VANILLA
¼ CUP UNSWEETENED COCOA POWDER	CHOPPED WALNUTS (OPT.)

Bring margarine, buttermilk, and cocoa powder to boil in a medium saucepan. Remove pan from heat. Beat in powdered sugar and vanilla; while still warm pour on cake. Top with nuts, if desired.

Note: Bake this cake on the day a family member sees the first sign of spring. This cake and frosting freeze well.

Makes 12 servings

Jiffy Salad

1 SMALL HEAD LETTUCE

2 TO 3 HARD-BOILED EGGS

Dressing

¼ TEASPOON SALT

¼ TEASPOON PEPPER

¼ CUP VEGETABLE OIL

2 TABLESPOONS VINEGAR

1 TEASPOON SOY SAUCE

1 TABLESPOON CHOPPED FRESH
    PARSLEY

¼ CUP GRATED PARMESAN CHEESE

Wash and shred lettuce; put in a salad bowl. Chop hard-boiled eggs; add to lettuce. Mix remaining ingredients for Dressing. Toss lettuce, eggs, and dressing.

Makes 4 servings

Cranberry Cream Salad

1 CUP HEAVY WHIPPING CREAM,
    CHILLED

3 TABLESPOONS SUGAR

2 3-OUNCE PACKAGES CREAM CHEESE

1 16-OUNCE CAN WHOLE CRANBERRY
    SAUCE

1 8-OUNCE CAN CRUSHED PINEAPPLE,
    DRAINED

Whip cream and sugar in a chilled bowl until stiff peaks form. Mix in remaining ingredients. Pour into a loaf pan and freeze. To serve, thaw slightly and cut into slices. Serve as a dessert or salad on lettuce leaves.

Makes 8 to 10 servings

Cinnamon Applesauce Salad

2 3-OUNCE PACKAGES LEMON GELATIN

½ CUP RED HOTS (CINNAMON OR
    CANDY IMPERIALS)

3 CUPS BOILING WATER

2 CUPS UNSWEETENED APPLESAUCE

1 TABLESPOON LEMON JUICE

DASH OF SALT

Dissolve gelatin and Red Hots in 3 cups boiling water, stirring until they dissolve. Stir in applesauce, lemon juice, and salt. Chill until set in a square 8x8x1½-inch pan or gelatin mold.

Makes 9 servings

Frozen Fruit Medley

1 17-OUNCE CAN APRICOTS (RESERVE THE SYRUP)

1 20-OUNCE CAN UNSWEETENED CRUSHED PINEAPPLE (RESERVE THE JUICE)

1 CUP COMBINED JUICE/SYRUP DRAINED FROM APRICOTS AND PINEAPPLE

½ CUP SUGAR

1 16-OUNCE PACKAGE UNSWEETENED, WHOLE FROZEN STRAWBERRIES

3 RIPE BANANAS, SLICED

1 6-OUNCE CAN FROZEN ORANGE-JUICE CONCENTRATE

2 TABLESPOONS LEMON JUICE

Drain apricots and pineapple, reserving 1 cup of combined syrup/juice. Cook the syrup/juice and sugar over medium heat about 5 minutes, stirring until sugar dissolves. Partially thaw strawberries until they can be separated. Add the apricots, pineapple, strawberries, sliced bananas, syrup/juice misture, sugar, orange-juice concentrate and lemon juice to the blender one at a time. Cover and puree until smooth and slightly chunky; then pour each batch of fruit mixture into a large bowl. When all fruit has been blended, stir together. Line 30 muffin cups with paper baking cups. Ladle fruit mixture into paper cups. Freeze until solid.

When frozen, turn over muffin tins, and punch out frozen fruit cups with your thumb. Package frozen fruit cups in freezer bags. Remove cups from freezer 20 minutes before serving as a salad or dessert.

Note: Put ice-cream sticks in each cup before freezing to make sherbet treats.

Makes 30 fruit cups

Hot Spiced Fruit

1 16-OUNCE CAN SLICED PEACHES
    WITH SYRUP
1 16-OUNCE CAN PEAR HALVES WITH
    SYRUP
1 15-OUNCE CAN PINEAPPLE CHUNKS
    WITH SYRUP

½ CUP ORANGE MARMALADE
1 3-INCH CINNAMON STICK
½ TEASPOON GROUND NUTMEG
¼ TEASPOON GROUND CLOVES

Mix all the ingredients with their liquids in a large saucepan. Bring to a boil; reduce heat. Cover and simmer 1 hour. Try fixing this in a Crock-Pot. Imagine the aroma!

Note: Eat this warm as a fruit sauce over ice cream or even served over sliced ham.

Makes 12 servings

Smoky Corn Chowder

½ CUP CHOPPED YELLOW ONION
4 TABLESPOONS BUTTER OR
    MARGARINE
¼ CUP ALL-PURPOSE FLOUR
1¼ TEASPOONS SALT
¼ TEASPOON PEPPER
4 CUPS MILK (WHOLE, 2%, OR SKIM)

1 17-OUNCE CAN WHOLE-KERNEL
    CORN, DRAINED
4 SMOKED SAUSAGE LINKS, SLICED
    (6-OUNCE PACKAGE)
1 8-OUNCE CAN LIMA BEANS (OPT.)

In a saucepan, sauté onion in butter or margerine until tender but not brown, about 3 to 5 minutes. Stir in flour, salt, and pepper. Add milk all at once. Bring to a boil, stirring constantly until thick and bubbly, about 1 minute. Stir in corn, sausage, and lima beans. Reduce heat; simmer 10 minutes.

Note: Spread a picnic blanket on the floor, and have a family picnic in front of the fireplace on a winter night. Serve Smoky Corn Chowder with fresh-baked bread. Toast marshmallows for dessert.

Makes 6 servings

Salsa de Lentejas

⅔ CUP CHOPPED ONION

1 SCANT TEASPOON (1 SMALL CLOVE) MINCED GARLIC

1 TABLESPOON VEGETABLE OIL

¾ CUP DRIED LENTILS, WASHED

2 CUPS WATER

2 BEEF BOUILLON CUBES

⅛ TEASPOON GROUND CAYENNE PEPPER

⅛ TEASPOON FRESHLY GROUND BLACK PEPPER

½ TEASPOON DRIED BASIL LEAVES, CRUMBLED

½ TEASPOON DRIED OREGANO LEAVES, CRUMBLED

2 TEASPOONS WHITE VINEGAR

1 8-OUNCE CAN TOMATO SAUCE

1 6-OUNCE CAN TOMATO PASTE

In a large saucepan, sauté onion and garlic in vegetable oil for about 5 minutes. Add lentils, water, beef bouillon cubes, cayenne, and black pepper. Cover and simmer for 30 minutes. Add basil, oregano, vinegar, tomato sauce, and tomato paste, and simmer uncovered about 1 hour, stirring occasionally.

Note: This is a tasty but hot dish!

Makes 5 servings

VEGETABLES

Twice-Baked Potatoes Deluxe

6 BAKING POTATOES

SALT AND PEPPER

MARGARINE OR BUTTER

MILK (WHOLE, 2%, OR SKIM)

¼ CUP CHOPPED ONION

¾ CUP GRATED CHEDDAR CHEESE

¾ CUP GRATED MONTEREY JACK CHEESE

1 BOX FROZEN, CHOPPED SPINACH, THAWED AND SQUEEZED DRY

Wash, prick, and bake 6 baking potatoes in a preheated 400°F oven for 1 hour. While potatoes are still hot, slice each potato in half lengthwise. Carefully scoop pulp into a large mixing bowl, leaving a thin shell. Mash potatoes, adding salt, pepper, margarine or butter to taste, and milk as needed. Stir in onion, cheddar, and Monterey Jack cheeses and spinach. Spoon potato mixture back into the shells.

Bake potato halves in a preheated 400°F oven for 20 minutes or until lightly browned. Serve immediately. Or freeze potatoes before reheating them. To serve potatoes, remove as many as needed. Allow to thaw, place on a rimmed cookie sheet or in a baking dish. Bake in a preheated 400°F oven about 20 minutes or until lightly browned.

Makes 12 servings

Fresh-Baked Asparagus

1 TO 1½ POUNDS FRESH ASPARAGUS
SALT AND PEPPER (LEMON PEPPER, IF
    DESIRED)
3 TABLESPOONS BUTTER

Rinse asparagus, and trim off rough ends. Place spears in one or two layers in a baking pan. Sprinkle with salt and pepper, and dot with butter. Cover with foil, and bake 30 minutes in a preheated oven at 300°F. The asparagus will be crunchy and will not lose color.

Makes 6 to 8 servings

Marinated Veggies

1 LARGE STALK FRESH BROCCOLI
1 3½-OUNCE CAN MEDIUM, PITTED
    BLACK OLIVES, DRAINED
1 16-OUNCE CAN GREEN BEANS,
    DRAINED
1 16-OUNCE CAN JULIENNED CARROTS,
    DRAINED
6 HALVED, CHERRY TOMATOES
¼ POUND SLICED, FRESH MUSHROOMS

Marinade
1 CUP CIDER VINEGAR
1 CUP SALAD OIL
1 MINCED, LARGE GARLIC CLOVE
¾ TEASPOON DRIED BASIL LEAVES
¾ TEASPOON DRIED OREGANO LEAVES
¾ TEASPOON SALT
¼ TEASPOON PEPPER
½ MINCED, SMALL ONION

Chop broccoli florets and a small portion of the upper stalk. Steam broccoli 5 minutes or until slightly crisp. Combine broccoli and remaining vegetables in a 2-quart casserole dish.

Mix Marinade in a small saucepan, bring to a boil, reduce heat, and simmer for 10 minutes. Pour Marinade over vegetables, toss, and refrigerate for several hours until chilled.

Note: Add your favorite cooked, small pasta for a Presto Pasta Salad.

Makes 12 servings

❑

CHAPTER 9

Post-Game Review: Adapting the Once-a-Month Method

❑

CHOOSING RECIPES

Once you've tried *Once-a-Month Cooking,* you may want to adapt it to your own recipes. The following suggestions will help you set up your system.

Choose dishes that freeze well. (See the section on freezer storage tips in Chapter 10.) Take into consideration that it's not safe to thaw meat, work with it, leave it raw, and then refreeze it. You must cook meat before freezing it again. But if you buy fresh meat, you can add ingredients and freeze the meat raw.

Start with your family's favorite recipes rather than exotic, new dishes. Or test recipes before you create your own plan. Be sure to pick simple recipes rather than ones that require many complicated steps. You need to keep your assembly order and food preparation as simple as possible. Otherwise, you'll be defeating your purpose of saving time.

Make sure you have a nice variety of recipes. You don't want to serve similar entrées too close together, such as two stews or three creamy noodle casseroles. If you don't mind eating the same dish twice in a month, double the recipe for a favorite entrée, divide it in half, and freeze it. You may also want to consider dishes that could be used for both lunch and dinner or could be taken to work and reheated in a microwave oven.

If you enjoy sharing food with others, choose some dishes that work well for company or could be taken to someone who is sick or has a special need.

After you decide what recipes you want to try, divide them into groups such as chicken, beef, fish, pork, meatless, or miscellaneous. This will show you how many recipes you have in each category. You may have too many chicken dishes or casseroles and need to balance your recipes by adding other kinds of meats or different types of dishes.

You may want to set up your system for only a week's worth of dishes rather than two weeks or a month. Or you may want to spread out the process, preparing all the dishes in a category at the same time—all the beef recipes in one afternoon, for example, and all the recipes in another category the next day.

Finally, make sure the ingredients called for in the recipes fit your budget. Some meats, especially fish, can be expensive.

MAKING A MENU CALENDAR

First, reproduce and use the blank calendar we've included in this chapter. Record names of recipes on it in pencil, so if you need to you can move them around.

Next, check your schedule for days the family will be away from home and won't need meals; cross off those dates. Take into account the nights you'll need to prepare something quick because you or your kids have meetings or activities. Pencil in easy-to-prepare dishes for those times. Make note of holidays or special occasions, such as a birthday or anniversary, which will require special planning.

Organize your recipes by category, such as beef, chicken, or miscellaneous, before filling out the menu calendar. Make sure you will serve a variety of entrées for each week.

If you plan to have company, select the recipes you would use for the occasion, and write these entrées on the appropriate dates. Do the same with dishes you want to take to a friend or to a potluck dinner. For dates when the adults will be away but the kids will be eating at home, choose dishes the children like and they or a baby-sitter can easily finish preparing.

If some dishes suit a particular day of the week, such as quiche on Sunday, add those recipes to the appropriate days. Then complete the calendar with your recipes.

Perhaps you may want to create your own plan without considering your schedule or special occasions. You just want to prepare two weeks or a month of meals at once and have them in your freezer. If you do that, you may still want to fill out a calendar so you have a variety of meals scheduled. It's also a way to keep track of the ones you've made. Check them off as you serve them to your family.

FIGURING SHOPPING AND STAPLES LISTS

Now use your recipes to compile your shopping and staples lists. You'll need a sheet of paper for each list. It may help to categorize your grocery list with the same headings we've used: Canned Goods; Grains, Pasta, and Rice; Dry Ingredients and Seasonings; Frozen Foods; Dairy Products; Meat and Poultry; and Produce.

You can also categorize your list by aisles or areas in your favorite supermarket. If you don't want to recopy your list, you can categorize by highlighting items with different colored marking pens: pink for produce, brown for meat, green for canned goods, and yellow for bakery.

To figure what food you'll need, check ingredients in each recipe, and record all the items on either the grocery shopping or staples lists. For example, if a recipe calls for cinnamon and you already have it, put it on the staples list. But add it to the shopping list if you don't have it. If 2½ pounds of chicken pieces are required, put them on the shopping list. For items needed for more than one recipe, such as onions, ground beef, or tomato sauce, keep a running tally of quantities needed, and then figure the total. (See Equivalent Measures in Chapter 10 for how to convert size of portions.)

Finally, be sure to list freezer bags or containers you will need in order to freeze each entrée. Then add the ones you'll need to your shopping list.

SETTING UP AN ASSEMBLY ORDER

Once you've filled in your calendar, check instructions in The Day Before Cooking Day and Cooking Day Assembly Order for the two-week and one-month plans to help you make out your own assembly order.

Copy your recipes on large, blank index cards. Then spread the recipes on a table and arrange them in an order that will flow well when you're preparing them. Group recipes that use similar ingredients, particularly meats.

Once you have your recipes in order, go through each one, tallying the total amount of each food item you'll need to process: how many onions to chop, carrots to shred, or ground beef to brown.

When you write out the assembly order, try to work with two or three recipes in the same category at a time, such as all the ground beef recipes or all the chicken. Record all the ingredients you'll need to store or freeze until the accompanying dishes are served. List any tasks you'll need to do the day before cooking day, such as cooking all the chicken or soaking pinto beans. You may also want to plan to do most of the chopping, grating, shredding, and slicing tasks the day before cooking day.

Then make out an assembly order with directions for how to proceed from one recipe to the next. If you haven't scheduled the chopping and slicing tasks for the day before, plan to do them the first thing on cooking day. Recipes that require longer cooking, such as soups or stews, should also be started early in the day.

Make sure you'll have enough stove burners to cook dishes in a particular group at the same time. Whenever possible, combine steps for several dishes: Cook rice for two dishes; sauté all onions at once.

Continue through all the recipes until you have completed your assembly order. Allow for time between groups of recipes so you can take some breaks.

EVALUATING YOUR PLAN

The first time you try your own plan, take a few extra minutes to write out any corrections in the recipes or procedures. That way, the next time you cook, it will go even more smoothly.

The following suggestions will help you revise your plan:

- Correct the order of tasks if they weren't easy to follow or in the right order. If you would do any part of the procedure differently, state what you would do.
- If you should have prepared some dishes sooner or later in the process, make note of it.
- Rework your plan if you had too many or too few dishes to prepare at once.
- Write out new directions if they were difficult to follow in any of the sections.
- If necessary, correct "ingredients needed" on your shopping list.

MENU CALENDAR

SUN.	MON.	TUES.	WED.	THURS.	FRI.	SAT.

❑

Equipment: Special Help

❑

EQUIVALENT MEASURES

1 tablespoon = 3 teaspoons, ½ fluid ounce

2 tablespoons = 1 fluid ounce

4 tablespoons = ¼ cup

5⅓ tablespoons = ⅓ cup

8 tablespoons = ½ cup

12 tablespoons = ¾ cup

16 tablespoons = 1 cup

1 cup = ½ pint or 8 fluid ounces

2 cups = 1 pint

2 pints = 1 quart

16 cups = 4 quarts or 1 liquid gallon

1 pound lean ground beef or sausage browned and drained = 2½ cups

1 pound cubed ham = 3 cups

1 cooked, deboned whole chicken (about 4 pounds) diced = 4½ cups

1 pound boneless, skinless chicken cooked and diced = 2¾ cups

1 medium yellow onion, chopped = 1¼ cups

1 medium yellow onion, chopped and sautéed = ¾ cup

1 medium green pepper, chopped = 1 cup
1 pound cheese, grated = 4 cups
3 ounces fresh mushrooms, sliced = 1 cup
1 pound zucchini, diced = 1½ cups
1 medium clove garlic, minced = 1 teaspoon

MORE FREEZER STORAGE TIPS

Frozen foods keep their natural color, flavor, and nutritive qualities better than canned or dried foods. Freezing also stops the bacterial action in fresh food that causes it to spoil.

Food kept in the freezer too long may not taste right, but it shouldn't make you sick. However, it's not safe to thaw food, especially meat, and then refreeze it without first cooking it.

Freezing food in moisture-proof containers with airtight lids or seals will help it keep its color and flavor much longer. You'll get the best results with products made for freezer use: plastic containers with lids; heavy aluminum foil; heavy plastic bags; freezer wraps and tape. Glass jars with lids (leave head space for the food to expand when it freezes) also work well.

Avoid using regular waxed paper; lightweight aluminum foil; regular plastic wrap or cellophane; cartons from cottage cheese, ice cream, or milk; ordinary butcher paper; the plastic film used on packaged meats; or plastic produce bags from the supermarket.

Follow these helpful hints for freezing foods:

Freeze food quickly to 0° or below.

Post a dated list of food on the freezer door, and keep it current.

Use frozen food within 1 month to 6 weeks. Some seasonings become stronger while frozen, and some weaker. The degree of change is minimized if food is not left frozen too long.

Thaw, heat, and serve food in rapid succession.

Allow hot foods to cool to room temperature before freezing, then freeze them immediately.

Blanch or precook vegetables and drain them before freezing to stop enzyme action and to keep them from becoming discolored and mushy. Drain blanched vegetables before freezing them.

Thaw foods in the refrigerator or microwave whenever possible. Thawing in the refrigerator will take twice as long as on the counter, but it's much safer. Thawing time will vary according to the thickness or quantity of food in the container.

So many foods freeze well that it's more helpful to ask what doesn't freeze well than what does. Don't freeze the following foods. They will change color, texture, or separate in some way during the freezing or thawing process:

> Raw salad vegetables (such as lettuce, radishes, tomatoes)
> Raw eggs in their shells or hard-boiled eggs
> Raw potatoes or boiled white potatoes (they turn black)
> Commercial cottage cheese
> Gelatin salads or desserts
> Icing made with egg whites, boiled frostings, or cakes with cream fillings
> Instant rice (it dissolves and becomes too mushy) You can freeze regular cooked rice
> Custard pies, cream pies, or pies with meringue

USING THE COMPUTER

Based on the book *Once-a-Month Cooking,* this CD-ROM, produced by Lifestyle Software Group, the industry leader in cookbook software, further streamlines the process for the busy family.

The program takes the *Once-a-Month Cooking* method of cooking a month's dinner entrées (or two weeks' dinner entrées) in a day and freezing them, and simplifies the process with the aid of computer technology. The program takes the book's easy-to-follow meal plans and recipes, time-saving and freezer-storage tips, and grocery shopping strategies, and adds video clips to the preparation guides. Unlike the book, the CD-ROM allows the cook to calculate the caloric and nutritional value of meals, adjust recipes to fit the number of portions desired, and print out recipes, shopping lists, and assembly orders.

How can you add your own recipes to the *Once-a-Month Cooking* system on CD-ROM? Once you have used and grown comfortable with the *Once-a-Month Cooking* system on CD-ROM, you may adapt the system to your own recipes with the help of additional software, the Micro-Kitchen Companion by Lifestyle Software. You can scan or type in your own recipes, and the Micro-Kitchen Companion will generate your shopping list. You then must develop an assembly order, using tips from the CD-ROM as your guide.

System requirements: Microsoft Windows 3.1 or higher, Windows 95 compatible; 8 MG RAM, 8 MG hard disk space available; 2X CD-ROM or better; 16-bit sound.

The software is available at software outlets. Or you may contact Lifestyle Software Group, 2155 Old Moultric Road, St. Augustine, Florida 32086-5125. Phone 904-794-7070. lsg@lifeware.com. http://www.lifeware.com.

INDEX

❑